D1126570

AFRICA
SOUTH OF THE SAHARA

CAMBRIDGE BOOKS ON THE HISTORY OF AFRICA

An Introduction to the History of West Africa
by J. D. FAGE

An Introduction to the History of East Africa
by ZOE MARSH and G. W. KINGSNORTH

Central and Southern Africa
by S. V. LUMB

AFRICA
SOUTH OF THE SAHARA

BY

G. W. KINGSNORTH

CAMBRIDGE
AT THE UNIVERSITY PRESS
1962

PUBLISHED BY

THE SYNDICS OF THE CAMBRIDGE UNIVERSITY PRESS

Bentley House, 200 Euston Road, London, N.W.1

American Branch: 32 East 57th Street, New York 22, N.Y.

West African Office: P.O. Box 33, Ibadan, Nigeria

©

CAMBRIDGE UNIVERSITY PRESS

1962

ADLARD AND SON LTD., DORKING

CONTENTS

47904

LIST OF MAPS

PREFACE

Today, Africa south of the Sahara is changing at a tremendous speed. The change is a general one; it is not confined to any one territory or group of territories. And what is true of Africa today has been true, in varying degrees, at other stages in its history, so that we can only see the different parts of the continent in their true perspective by knowing something of the general history of Africa as well. This book is an attempt to show the history of Africa south of the Sahara as a whole, so that each part of the continent may be seen as part of the general pattern of development instead of as an isolated unit. But, at the same time, the text has been arranged so that the reader who wishes to follow the history of any particular region will be able to do so without difficulty. This arrangement also enables teachers to avoid the fault of going over material which is already known.

This is not a book for the specialist. It is an introductory outline and not a detailed study. It is particularly intended for use in secondary schools as a background to the Cambridge Overseas School Certificate syllabus on Tropical Africa, but it should also prove useful at the Intermediate level, for the English is simple without being childish. If I have been successful in my attempt to make it interesting, and not just a dull catalogue of facts, it may also prove suitable for the general reader who wants a brief, readable account of Africa past and present.

Thanks are due to the many people who have helped and encouraged me in writing this book, but I am particularly grateful to my friend and colleague, Mr David Odongo, upon whose advice and criticism I have greatly relied, and to Dr. J. D. Fage, editor of the *Journal of African History*, whose generous help has enabled me to avoid many of the dangers which beset a book such as this. Sincere thanks are also due to Mr P. T. C. Lewin for his cheerful help in checking the proofs.

G. W. K.

KIKUYU, KENYA
August 1960

PART I

EARLY HISTORY

INTRODUCTION

The difference between the history of Africa north and south of the Sahara is tremendous. The north coast contained one of the earliest civilised countries of which we have any definite knowledge. Africa south of the Sahara, on the other hand, was one of the last areas to come into contact with the civilisations of other parts of the world.

In the first part of this book we shall look at the early history of the people south of the Sahara, and see how much they were influenced by the people of the north.

CHAPTER I

THE INFLUENCE OF NORTH AFRICA

THE MEDITERRANEAN CIVILISATIONS

The Egyptians

Five thousand years ago one of the most advanced people in the world lived in Africa. They were the Egyptians, who lived in the Nile Delta and along the Nile Valley up to the first cataract where the Aswan Dam now stands. The life of a rich Egyptian, even in those early days, was most comfortable. He would live beside the Nile in a brightly coloured house of brick and wood surrounded by a walled garden. Here his children splashed and played in ornamental pools, while the nobleman himself rested beneath the shady trees playing at draughts, listening to music, or watching his dancers or his children. The rulers, or Pharaohs, of Egypt lived in even greater luxury in their splendid palaces where they were waited upon by hundreds of servants. The tomb of King Khufu, which is the Great Pyramid, still stands over the desert at Gizeh and gives us some idea of the wealth and authority of the Pharaohs. It towers nearly 500 feet above the ground, it contains nearly two and a half million blocks of limestone each weighing about two and a half tons, and it is said that it took 100,000 men twenty years to build. The Egyptians were not advanced only in their buildings. In their farming they used a plough pulled by oxen instead of a hoe wielded by hand, and in the arts their painters, goldsmiths, potters and furniture makers reached a high standard of workmanship. In learning, not only could they read and write, but they also knew the simple rules of arithmetic based on the decimal system, besides having a considerable knowledge of medicine—including the use of castor oil! All these things, and more, were common in Egypt from 3000 B.C. To the east, along the banks of the Tigris and Euphrates, a similar standard of living had also been reached.

Later North African influences

Since that distant time, invaders, settlers and conquerors have come and gone. Usually they have assisted the process of development. Among the earliest were the Phoenician traders from Tyre and Sidon who founded Carthage about 822 B.C. and probably introduced the vine, the olive and the fig, besides several animals. Later, the Greeks, whose art and literature are still among the finest in the world, also made their contribution. They colonised Cyrene as early as 631 B.C., but their main influence was felt when Alexander the Great added Egypt to the Greek Empire in 332 B.C. and founded Alexandria, which was named after him. As a centre of learning, as a port, and as a place of sheer magnificence with its shining marble palace and huge lighthouse, Alexandria was the greatest city of the ancient world. Although the Greek rule collapsed when Mark Antony and Cleopatra were defeated by the Romans at the battle of Actium (31 B.C.), North Africa continued to develop, and numerous

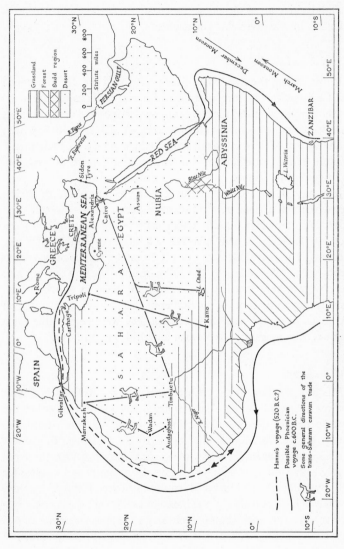

Map 1. North Africa up to the fall of the Roman Empire.

3

splendid cities grew up along the coasts of Algeria and Morocco, defended by the invincible Roman army.

Christian and Jewish influence

It was during the time when Rome controlled the Mediterranean that Christianity was born, and the message of Jesus spread throughout the Empire aided by the good communications which the Romans provided. By the end of the third century A.D. Christianity had been definitely established in North Africa which produced some of the greatest early Christians of whom the best known is probably St Augustine of Hippo.

Jews as well as Christians influenced the history of North Africa. Egypt was for a time (*c.* 1710–1550) overrun by a powerful confederation of mainly Semitic tribes called 'Hyksos', which means 'Foreign Rulers'. Much later the fall of Jerusalem in 587 B.C. encouraged Jewish settlement outside Palestine, and colonies spread throughout Egypt and along the coast, until by the first century A.D. there were a very considerable number of Jews in North Africa. Usually they settled among the Berber people peacefully as craftsmen and as farmers, although in Cyrenaica they were responsible for a major rebellion against the Roman authorities in A.D. 117.

The Arabs

Much of the flourishing civilisation which the Romans had built up was shattered by the Vandals from Europe who invaded the western part of the north coast in 439, but it was the Arabs who finally removed the Roman influence from North Africa. In 570 was born the prophet Mohammed, who successfully provided the Arab people with a religious faith which gave them a unity and a desire for military conquest that altered the course of African history. Inspired by their beliefs, and also by the hopes of rich booty, the Arab horsemen achieved an astonishingly rapid series of major victories. In 636 they conquered Syria, a year later they conquered Mesopotamia, in 639 they invaded Egypt, and three years later entered Alexandria.

By 702 they had conquered the whole north coast westwards to what is now Algeria and Morocco, and from here they crossed the straits and conquered most of Spain as well. For northern Africa these conquests were by no means disastrous. Since the downfall of the Roman Empire civilisation in Europe had gone backwards rapidly so that for the centuries following the Arab invasion the Muslim countries enjoyed a higher standard in the arts of peace than anywhere else. This high standard was shared by the people of North Africa. Further waves of Arab invaders came to the north coast in later centuries, and in the sixteenth century Egypt was conquered by the Turks. But, from the first Arab conquests until the French and British intervention in the nineteenth century, the main influence in North Africa was that of Islam.

THE CONNEXIONS OF THE NORTH WITH THE SOUTH

Factors limiting influence to the south

We have seen that Mediterranean Africa has shared in the advances of knowledge which have been made since the beginning of history and has sometimes led the way. How far has this affected the rest of Africa to the south?

For several reasons it has affected it only to a limited extent. In the first place the Sahara desert has never been an attractive trade route, and so most of North Africa's trade went by sea to Europe or by land to Syria. We shall see that for various reasons people did cross the desert from earliest times, but connexions along the Mediterranean were much simpler and much more common. A second obstacle which made connexions southwards difficult was the Equatorial forest stretching across the whole west coast to the centre of the continent. This was fertile and in some areas provided gold, but it was dense and, above all, it was unhealthy. In its dampness swarmed mosquitoes to kill invading man with malaria, and the tsetse fly to kill animals with sleeping sickness. Therefore the desert horsemen, who were prepared to risk the drought and sandstorms of the Sahara, still kept clear of the forest where attacks from man and from disease were more difficult to combat. The third obstacle was the Nile sudd. The Nile regularly provided soil in which the Egyptian farmer could plant his crops and a flood to water them. To some extent it also provided a means of travel by boat. Yet it was a limited means of travel, for above the present site of Aswan a series of cataracts lay across its course, and even more serious was the impenetrable tangle of weeds, or sudd, which completely blocked the river in the southern Sudan. Thus, although the Nile was vital to Egyptian agriculture, it was not so valuable as a route to the interior.

Early connexions between the north and south

But although Africa south of the Sahara has never been an easy place to reach it has not been entirely cut off from the north or from the rest of the world.

While by far the greater part of Egypt's trade went eastwards or along the Mediterranean, some of her goods and some of her ideas influenced regions to the south. Apart from her connexions with the Nubian kingdom of Meroe on her southern border, and with Abyssinia, her influence also reached as far south as the shores of Lake Victoria. Beads, carved stools, and various weapons from slings to battle-axes were traded here thousands of years ago, and the inhabitants of these areas may well have enjoyed some lively dancing to bands which used drums, xylophones and zithers of Egyptian origin. The first domestic animals such as oxen, sheep, goats and dogs also seem to have been introduced to the tropical parts of Africa from Egypt, but how all these articles reached the centre of the continent is far from clear.

It seems that it was the Egyptians too who organised the first circumnavigation of Africa in about 600 B.C., when they ordered a Phoenician captain to sail right round the continent from east to west. This took him about three years, but he seems to have completed his task and to have stopped on the way to sow and reap a grain crop in southern Africa. About a hundred years later, perhaps in 520 B.C., a Carthaginian explorer, Hanno, led a large fleet through the Straits of Gibraltar to explore southwards along the West

African coast. He started several trading bases and perhaps reached the Senegal.

In the Roman period exploration was continued. In 19 B.C. a Roman General, Septimus Flaccus, is said to have marched in three months from the region of Tripoli across the Sahara to the Sudan, and some years later another Roman explorer made a similar expedition, probably to the area of Lake Chad.

The Saharan trade

More important than these expeditions was the Saharan trade that grew, particularly in the Greek and Roman periods. In West Africa the Negro people south of the Sahara required salt, which the white people north of the Sahara provided in exchange for gold and slaves. Thus, a considerable trade developed across the desert, being greatly encouraged no doubt by the introduction of the camel, which was in general use by about the third century A.D. Long lines of these camels and of slaves would start from centres in the Sudan and move slowly northwards across the Sahara, stopping at oases on the way. Somewhere in the region of Morocco, Tunisia, or Egypt the journey would end, but after a while the camel drivers would turn their caravans towards the south again, bringing salt, copper, cloth, and various ornaments to the Negroes. The traders who crossed and recrossed the desert carried ideas and information as well as trading goods, and during the first few centuries A.D. some ideas about Christianity had reached the people south of the Niger. Ideas on building fortresses had reached them too. Northwards traders and explorers carried information about the geography of the Niger area. They told of lands to the south of the desert where rhinoceros swarmed, where crocodiles and hippopotami splashed in muddy rivers, a land where the vegetation was dense and rich and in whose forests gold was found.

East Africa

On the eastern side of Africa the main routes of exploration and trade were along the Nile or across the Indian Ocean.

The most interesting expedition along the Nile was in A.D. 66 when the Roman Emperor Nero became interested in the Nile sources and sent an expedition led by two centurions to explore up the river. Centurions were tough, and despite the heat and the mosquitoes, and the hostility of the Nile Negroes, they reached the junction of the Blue Nile and White Nile. At this point the sudd forced them to return, but it was a great achievement and until the nineteenth century no other white explorer penetrated so far.

The exploration of the Red Sea from Egypt began about 300 B.C. From here sailors continued into the Indian Ocean, exploring eastwards towards India and southwards along the African coast. In A.D. 45 a great step forward was made when the trader Hippalus discovered the use of the monsoon winds in the Indian Ocean: these would carry ships from the north-east in December and from the south-west in March, which resulted in the development of trade between India and Arabia and the east coast of Africa. By A.D. 60 Indian and Arab traders knew this coast as far south as Zanzibar. In general the traders to East Africa seem to have stayed on the coast, but there is an interesting story of one of them, Diogenes, who attempted to explore inland about A.D. 50. According to his own story he travelled inland for twenty-five days and reached a range of snow-capped mountains and two great lakes from which the Nile drew its water, but this must have been just guesswork because it would have been impossible to reach Lake Victoria in twenty-five days from the coast.

Summary

To sum up: when the Roman Empire fell the northern influence seems to have been as follows. In the west a steady trans-Saharan trade existed between the north and the Sudan, but this did not extend into the forest regions although no doubt it influenced them. On the eastern side Abyssinia had become a flourishing Christian state whose trade and influence extended not only northwards to Egypt and Arabia, but also a considerable depth into the interior of the continent, perhaps as far as Lake Rudolf. On the east coast—but only on the coast—a regular trade existed depending on the monsoons, the main commodities being spices, ivory and slaves.

But apart from these trading contacts the civilisations of northern Africa and the Middle East do not seem to have affected the rest of Tropical Africa. Trade, which has always been the great link between different peoples, did not develop with the interior, with the Congo, with Central Africa, or with the south. It did not do so because geographical factors made these regions too difficult to reach, and because it did not, and because these regions remained isolated for so long, most of Africa south of the Sahara developed slowly and independently, and our knowledge of that early development is small.

But in the next chapter we must try to piece together such knowledge as we have.

CHAPTER 2

EARLY CIVILISATIONS OF AFRICA SOUTH OF THE SAHARA

Every continent in the world contains a mixture of races, and Africa is no exception. There is no record of when the first men existed in the continent; we guess it from archaeological remains and from rock-drawings. Nor do we know exactly when other groups of people entered the continent and married with those already there. But from appearances, from languages, and from habits we can make some reasonable guesses about the very early history of Africa, and during the last thousand years—and on a few earlier occasions—we have some knowledge passed on by speech or in writing. Let us see what we can put together from these sources.

Recent investigations have upset many of the old ideas about the races and language groupings in Africa, especially in connexion with the use of the word 'Hamite' to describe some of the invading groups, and the whole question is now so uncertain that here it will be best simply to notice that the word 'Negro' is used to describe the tall, black, thick-lipped people of West Africa, and that the word

'Bantu' is used to describe a group of languages spoken by most of the people south of the 'Bantu line' shown on the map. These Bantu-speaking people are likely to have been an off-shoot of the West African Negroes who emigrated to the area of the Zambezi Valley and spread out from there in all directions, absorbing earlier residents as they did so. Other groupings of people are the Hottentots and Bushmen of South Africa, and the Pygmies of the Congo forest. Mention should also be made of the peoples speaking Semitic languages, whose original homes were in Syria and Arabia and whose influence has reached Africa by sea along the east coast, and by land across the Suez Isthmus. They became particularly important in East and North Africa after the Arab conquests of the seventh century.

If we try to discover the early history of these people we get into difficulties for there are no written records, but it is worth while to look at some of the knowledge we have.

SOUTHERN AND CENTRAL AFRICA

The Pygmies, Bushmen and Hottentots

The existence of the Pygmies was certainly known to the Pharaohs of Egypt 5000 years ago, when they were valued for their ability to imitate people. One Pharaoh gave very strict orders to his caravan leader about the care which a captured Pygmy was to receive, 'When he sleeps at night,' wrote the Pharaoh, 'appoint excellent people who shall sleep beside his tent. . . . My sovereignty desires to see this dwarf more than all the gifts of Sinai or Punt.' But of the Pygmies' general history very little is known.

In southern Africa, some of the early inhabitants were the Bushmen. They were hunters and nomads who lived in very rough and temporary shelters made of branches and usually situated near a water-hole. One of their most interesting characteristics was their great skill in painting and engraving on stone. Later on, perhaps in the fourteenth century, groups of Hottentot people entered southern

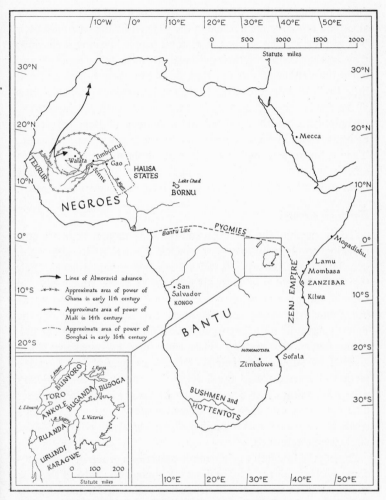

Map 2. Africa south of the Sahara in the centuries before the arrival of the Europeans.

Africa moving southwards along the west coast and then northwards along the east coast after reaching the Cape. The Bushmen did their best to prevent these groups of pastoral people invading their land; they attacked them with their poisoned arrows and they captured and killed their animals. But the Hottentots were better organised and little by little they forced the Bushmen into the less valuable areas of the dry interior. The Hottentots were cattle-keepers who lived in encampments which consisted of a number of huts that could easily be moved when the grass for the cattle and sheep was eaten. They seem to have made no serious attempts at cultivation, but in other ways they developed crafts of their own, such as the carving of wooden utensils and the weaving of mats and baskets from reeds.

Bantu kingdoms

To the north of the Bushmen and the Hottentots were the Bantu-speaking people, who may have reached Central Africa about A.D. 900. They cultivated crops as well as keeping domestic animals. Their typical settlement was probably not unlike those which are still common in many areas today, consisting of round mud and wattle huts roofed with grass, with their areas of cultivation nearby. To the Bantu people the most important factor in their society was the link of the family, clan or tribe. They were ruled by hereditary chiefs assisted by subordinate chiefs. Sometimes quarrels arose and a section of a tribe would break away to form a new or subsidiary tribe. Sometimes a strong chief would force his rule upon other different tribes, establishing his influence over a large area, and as a result of such conquests a number of comparatively powerful kingdoms were established.

During the fifteenth to eighteenth centuries a group of such kingdoms lay between the Zambezi and Limpopo Rivers, and the best known of them was the gold-producing realm of Monomotapa—a corruption of 'Mwene-mutapa' which some people think means 'Lord Hippopotamus' and others 'Lord of the (gold) mine'. The ruler of Monomotapa had so much respect from the first Portuguese who visited his kingdom that he was referred to as Emperor. Although his power was in decline in the sixteenth century he was still strong enough to prevent his kingdom being conquered by the Portuguese.

Another Bantu kingdom was that of Kongo. This covered a large area of the coast across the mouth of the Congo River (which was known by the Africans as the Zaire until it was renamed after the kingdom of Kongo) and stretched far inland. The royal capital city of Kongo lay over 150 miles inland. Whenever the king reviewed his army, he rode, according to one report, upon an elephant surrounded by slaves and nobles, and followed by a man whose special task was to talk loudly and continuously about the king's courage and bravery. How, or when, this kingdom of Kongo began we do not know, but it greatly impressed the Portuguese.

The region of the Great Lakes, which is roughly covered today by Uganda, was occupied by the Bachwezi—who were one of the Hima clans from the north—between the thirteenth and fifteenth centuries. They established the Kitwara empire. In the fifteenth and sixteenth centuries further invaders drove the Bachwezi southwards into the regions of Ankole, Ruanda, Urundi and Karagwe, and divided the northern part into the still surviving kingdoms of Bunyoro, Buganda, Toro and Busoga. At first Bunyoro was the most powerful of these kingdoms, but during the eighteenth century Buganda became stronger and conquered Busoga to the east as well as raiding northwards and southwards. By the middle of the nineteenth century Buganda had built up the most advanced society in Central Africa, ruled over by a king, called a Kabaka, who was assisted by chiefs who owed allegiance to him. The magnificence of the Kabaka, whose ceremonial costume consisted of a leopard skin and the traditional bark-cloth and beadwork of the Baganda, greatly impressed the first European travellers.

One of the mysteries of the early period of African history is the site of Great Zimbabwe, which means something like 'the great stone houses'. Generally the Bantu people built in mud and wattle, but between the Zambezi and the Limpopo there are hundreds of stone-built ruins, of which Great Zimbabwe is the most impressive. It consists of a ruined temple 34 feet high and 830 feet in circumference, and a fortress which stands on top of a rock 350 feet high. Between lies the 'Valley of Ruins'. These ruins were noticed by the Portuguese but no one is quite sure who built them. It has been suggested that they are very ancient (1200–900 B.C.) and were built by the Phoenicians and Egyptians, but it now seems fairly certain that they were the work of the Bantu about a thousand years ago.

WEST AFRICA

In West Africa there are two very different regions: the forested coastal belt which could not easily be penetrated, and the grassland area of the Sudan.

In the grassland area which borders the Sahara there were a succession of great territorial states or empires, which were started by invading groups of the lighter-skinned people from the North African settlements, or by Negroes who had learnt new methods of fighting from them. The chief advantage which these invaders had was the possession of horses and camels. Using these they managed to gain control over wide areas in the savannah region, but they never penetrated far into the forest, and their administration was often concerned only with the collection of taxes. As soon as their military strength declined these empires fell.

Ghana

The first of these empires which we know much about was that of Ghana. This seems to have been started, not by conquest but by the peaceful settlement of Berbers or Jews from the north coast in the second century. During the fourth century the descendants of these white settlers became rulers of the Negro people among whom they lived, until in about 770 they were overthrown by the Negro Soninke people. Stretching eastwards to the Niger bend, southwards to Senegal, and northwards into the Sahara, Ghana became a major focus for the desert caravans, and became very prosperous from its exports of gold obtained from the neighbouring district of Wangara. The method by which the Ghana merchants obtained the gold was interesting. They never spoke to the Mandingo people who mined it. Instead they just showed their own goods for sale on the river bank and withdrew until the Mandingo placed sufficient gold beside them. Then, the Ghana merchants would take the gold and the Mandingo miners would take the goods, each departing silently.

The downfall of Ghana resulted from the hostility of the Berber tribes to the north, who were united in 1042 by one of the great characters in African history—Ibn Yasin. He started as a Muslim missionary with very strict ideas, and finished by leading a holy war with the purpose of conquering and converting the people of Morocco and the Sudan. The success of his Berber followers, known as the Almoravids, was spectacular. Mounted on horses and camels, or else marching on foot with pikes and spears, this force of 30,000 men was the best disciplined army the Sudan had ever seen. They quickly conquered it, as well as Morocco, and finally forced their way into Spain. Among their conquests in the Sudan was Ghana, which was conquered in 1076, but the Almoravids—like many conquerors—found it easier to conquer than to hold, and in 1087 the Soninke kings of Ghana regained their independence. But Ghana never recovered its former glory. Provinces began to break away into independent kingdoms, and the once proud and mighty kings now only ruled effectively over a few towns. The capital city of Ghana was taken by the Sosso in 1203 and was destroyed by the Mali emperor in 1240, but by then most of the population had already moved northwards to start a new trading centre at Walata.

Mali

The Mali (or Melle) empire exceeded that of Ghana in size, magnificence and wealth. Its rise was due to the reign of King Sundiata who built it from the comparatively small Mandingo state of Kangaba whose rulers had earlier become Muslims. In 1235 he defeated the Sosso emperor and annexed his empire which lay to the north. Then he destroyed Ghana and built himself a new capital city of Mali which became the richest of the western Sudan. His empire continued to expand until his successors exercised authority from

Tekruru in the west to Gao in the east. Like Ghana, the Mali empire drew its wealth from the trans-Saharan trade which depended on obtaining gold and slaves from further south. The attention of the whole civilised western world was drawn to this Negro kingdom of Mali when, in 1324, its ruler Mansa Musa set out across the desert on a pilgrimage to Mecca. His wealth and splendour staggered everyone. In front of him went 500 slaves, each carrying a heavy staff of gold; behind him came 100 camels each carrying 300 lb. of gold; in fact he showered so much gold in trade and presents during his journey that its value in Egypt fell sharply and for twelve years afterwards the people of Cairo were still talking of him with admiration. After the reign of Mansa Musa the Mali empire declined, and by the sixteenth century its rulers were again left with only the state of Kangaba.

Songhai

In the later fifteenth century the Songhai empire, with its capital at Gao on the middle Niger, had started to expand as a result of a series of conquests by King Sonni Ali (1464-92), whose family had previously gained control over the Songhai people of the middle Niger. By the time of his death Sonni Ali had captured the great commercial centres of Timbuctu and Jenne. He had also gained a large fortune and a reputation for cruelty. Soon after his death his throne was taken by one of his Soninke generals who was a sincere Muslim and took the title of 'Askia', calling himself Mohammed I. Not only did he make a splendid pilgrimage to Mecca as Mansa Musa had done in the previous century; he also started a policy of conquest, which was so successful that it resulted in the capture of a large part of the remaining Mali empire in the west, the Hausa states in the east, and the salt mines of Taghaza in the desert to the north. But the most remarkable feature of the empire that Askia Mohammed I had gained was the peace and order which were maintained within it. Trade, both across the desert and with the vital gold-producing regions to the south, flourished; banking was encouraged; a police system was set up; a university of high academic standing was established at Timbuctu; the wealthy lived in stone houses complete with libraries and with stables for their horses— even Mansa Musa's reign had not seen so much prosperity and so many of the fruits of peace. But in 1528 the long rule of Askia Mohammed I—'the greatest monarch that ever ruled in the western Sudan'—ended in tragedy, when the blind old man was exiled by his rebellious sons to an island in the Niger where he died amid the frogs and mosquitoes of its swamps. Thereafter the story of the Songhai empire is one of decline, which ended when an army from Morocco, armed with guns which the Songhai had not seen before, defeated the Askia's army near Gao in 1591.

The aim of the Moroccans was to gain control of the gold from West Africa, but they were disappointed. As the Songhai army, which had maintained peace in the Sudan, collapsed, its subject peoples rebelled, and in the resulting chaos trade withered and so did the gold supply. The Moroccan army was not large enough to restore order or conquer the gold-producing lands of the forest, and could do little more than hold the main centres of Gao, Timbuctu and Jenne. Meanwhile Europeans had reached the west coast by sea and the gold, which had once flowed only to the north, began to find another outlet towards the coast. By 1618 the Moroccan attempt to hold the Sudan was officially abandoned.

Other states

Before leaving the Sudan we should also notice the important states of Bornu and the seven senior Hausa states in the east. These emerged in the tenth century, and the Hausa language is now in general use for trade throughout the Sudan. Politically these states were never very strong, and the Fulani gained control over them in the early nineteenth century and placed their main towns under Fulani emirs paying tribute to Sokoto.

The empires of the Sudan were at first stronger and better organised than those of the forest people to the south with whom they traded in gold and slaves. But when the Europeans began trading on the coast from the fifteenth century the position changed.

Raiding and conquest increased in scale as a result of the guns which had been brought in, and we shall see how large forest states began to develop that were similar in many ways to those of the Sudan.

EAST AFRICA

The Zenj empire

We have seen that traders came to the east coast of Africa from very early times, and that from the discovery of the monsoons by Hippalus in A.D. 45 trade had developed especially with India and Arabia. At first there seems to have been no question of settlement by these traders; they just came and went according to the winds. Between the second and seventh centuries this trade decreased, partly due to a decline in Arab prosperity and partly due to the invasions of the Bantu peoples into the coastal districts. But from the seventh century, following the rise of Islam, groups of rebel Arabs began to settle on the Lamu archipelago and at various points southwards along the coast. A major group of settlements has been doubtfully attributed to a Persian, Hasan bin Ali, who with his seven sons, is said to have founded several towns including Mombasa and Kilwa, which became the most important settlement on the coast. The start of the Zenj empire is usually dated from the arrival of Hasan bin Ali and his sons in 975.

The Zenj empire extended southwards to Sofala and northwards to Mogadishu, and was really a series of almost independent coastal towns, despite the authority which Kilwa claimed over the others. Most, like Kilwa, Zanzibar, and Mombasa, were built on islands for defence from the coastal Africans and from one another, for there was a great deal of rivalry between them. The islands also made suitable sites for the sea-borne trade on which they depended. The chief exports were still slaves and ivory, and through Sofala came considerable quantities of gold from inland. In return for these commodities beads, glass, metal-work, and cloth were imported. The settlements were confined to the coast and no attempt was made to conquer or occupy the interior. Caravans had to make journeys inland in order to obtain the ivory and slaves, but their purpose was trade, not conquest.

We have several descriptions of life in these coastal towns during the Zenj empire, and from them it is clear that the Sultans who governed them lived in considerable luxury. They had stone-built palaces and were attended by a multitude of slaves; they ate tremendous quantities of food, wore gorgeous robes, and were treated with immense respect. Their ways were copied on a less expensive scale by their Arab and Indian subjects, who intermarried with the Africans on the coast to form the Swahili people. On the whole, although fighting did occur with the coastal tribes, it does not seem to have been bitter or prolonged and we may picture life in these coastal towns as hot, lazy, and luxurious, the main interests being trade and rivalry with some other family or settlement. Everything depended on the caravans and the labour of slaves, and even for them life may not have been as bad as might be imagined for kindly treatment of them was part of the Muslim faith.

By 1498, when the Portuguese arrived, the Arab, and to a lesser extent the Persian and Indian, influence on the coast had already made important differences to African life there. Besides the articles of trade which they brought they also introduced the Muslim faith, which is still strong in the coastal districts, and the art of building in stone.

By the fifteenth century we may therefore think of southern Africa as occupied by the semi-nomadic pastoral Hottentots, and Central Africa as occupied by the Bantu, some of whom had organised themselves into powerful kingdoms while others were grouped in strong tribes which were tending to expand southwards. In the Sudan and on the east coast, which were more open to outside influences, a high degree of civilisation had been reached.

It was at this point in Africa's history that the European influence began to be felt along the coastlines south of the Sahara.

PART II

EUROPE AND THE COAST

INTRODUCTION

In the fifteenth century a new influence came to Africa when European ships explored its coastline and began to trade. Four centuries later this led to the control of a large part of Africa by European governments, but at first European contacts were, with very few exceptions, confined to the coast. There were good reasons for this. The traders from Europe came by sea and could obtain from the coastal people the main articles they required—gold and slaves. They had no wish, therefore, to penetrate inland where the rivers were unnavigable, where climate and disease might kill, and where the coastal forest in the west and the waterless thorn-scrub in the east made travel a nightmare, quite apart from the hostility and opposition they were likely to meet. And so for centuries there was little attempt to explore the interior by Europeans and there was no attempt to occupy it.

In this part of the book we shall see the effects which the early European coastal trade had.

CHAPTER 3

THE FIRST COASTAL CONTACTS

EUROPEAN TRADE WITH THE EAST

During the Middle Ages the richer people of Europe wanted a number of goods which could only be obtained from the East. The chief of these was spices, which were needed for preserving meat during winter months as well as for flavouring food. Other eastern commodities were silk, sugar and ivory. After passing through the hands of many merchants these commodities, which came originally from the East Indies, China, India or East Africa, found their way by land and sea to the markets at the eastern end of the Mediterranean. By that time they cost much more than their original producer had sold them for, because each trader and each country had taken a profit or toll. Until it reached the Mediterranean this trade was almost entirely managed by Muslims, who controlled the markets of Egypt, Syria and Asia Minor, as well as the sea routes across the Indian Ocean. But the carrying of eastern goods along the Mediterranean and their distribution to Europe were controlled by merchants from the Italian cities of Genoa and, from the fourteenth century, Venice. At least one attempt had been made by the Genoese in the thirteenth century to reach the east by sailing round Africa, because they realised that the sea route would cut out most of the middlemen and all the tolls, thus enabling them to sell the eastern goods more cheaply than those purchased from the Muslims, but those who set out on this expedition were never seen again.

Their disappearance served to increase the fear of the Atlantic, or 'Green Sea of Darkness', which people in Europe felt. The secrets of the Phoenician circumnavigation and of Hanno's voyage were unknown. The Atlantic Ocean seemed to Europe in the Middle Ages to be the margin of the world. If you attempted to cross it people thought you would perish. Sail south of the wind-swept Cape Bojador and they thought you would find a region where the sea boiled, where monsters lurked, and where white men turned black. Christian and Muslim, European and Arab, were agreed that the idea of exploring the Atlantic was dangerous and foolish.

PORTUGUESE EXPLORATION

Prince Henry the Navigator and the sea route to the East

The man who did most to overcome these fears was Prince Henry the Navigator, who was a son of the king of Portugal. His country,

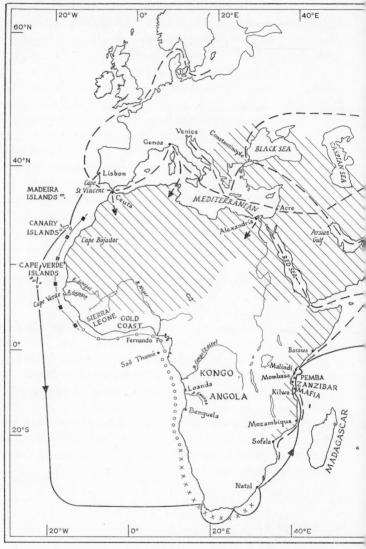

Map 3. Voyages of exploration and

22

Key:
- ▪——▪ Coast explored by Prince Henry's captains
- ○——○ Coast explored under Gomes's contract
- ○○○○○○ Coast explored by Diego Cam 1482-6
- × × × × × Coast explored by Diaz 1487
- ——➤ Voyage of Vasco da Gama 1497-8
- — — — Trade routes in 15th century
- ⫽⫽⫽ Areas of Muslim control in 15th century

CHINA
Silks, Ginger

JAPAN

INDIA
Pepper, Cotton, Sugar,
Precious stones

Goa

Calicut

CEYLON
Cinnamon,
Ivory

PHILIPPINE
ISLANDS

Malacca

SUMATRA

BORNEO

CELEBES

MOLUCCAS

EAST INDIES

JAVA

Cloves from Moluccas
Pepper from Java and Sumatra

..de routes in the fifteenth century.

23

like the rest of the Iberian peninsula, had been invaded in the eighth century by the Arabs from North Africa. By the middle of the thirteenth century nearly all the invaders had been driven out, and in 1415 the Portuguese carried the war into the enemy's country when they attacked the Arab town of Ceuta in North Africa. The young Prince Henry had begged his father to let him lead the attack and when the town had been taken he was made its Governor. But he did not stay there. His aims went far beyond the governorship of one Mediterranean town—he wanted to explore the coast of Africa by sea.

Why did he want to attempt this exploration when most of the other people of his time thought that he was quite mad? Certainly the hope of starting a profitable trade with the west coast was one reason. At Ceuta he must have seen the wealth in gold which came across the Sahara, and one of his main aims at first was to reach the source of this gold by sea. As time went on the hope grew that his ships might also reach the valuable markets of the Indian Ocean for which the Genoese had sought in vain. But Henry was much more than an adventurous business man. He was also a scholar to whom the unknown coast of Africa presented an interesting geographical problem, and he was a sincere Christian who hoped to convert the African people. There were also rumours that in Ethiopia there was a powerful Christian king, Prester John, whose help might be obtained against the Muslims. In fact there was a Christian king in this country and in the sixteenth century the Portuguese did ally with him, but he was not as powerful as people had hoped.

The process of exploration which Prince Henry encouraged had serious difficulties. We have already noticed the general fear of the Atlantic which existed. In addition to this the European ships of the early fifteenth century were clumsy wooden trading vessels with square-shaped sails which could not easily sail unless the wind came from nearly behind them. Such ships were not suitable for making their way along the coast of Africa. One of the achievements of the Portuguese was to modify the Arab lateen sail for their own use, thus producing a sailing ship which was partly eastern and partly western in its design. This development of a swifter, more manageable craft, which they called a 'caravel', made the exploration of the coast less difficult. Nevertheless, although the Portuguese probably had the best ships afloat by the end of the fifteenth century, life on board was still extremely uncomfortable. There was nowhere for the crew to sleep except on the decks, where rats and cockroaches swarmed and nibbled at the sleepers' feet. Food consisted of salted meat and ship's biscuits, which were usually as hard as iron and full of weevils. Water went bad after a short time at sea and formed a nasty-looking scum on top; needless to say most people preferred to drink wine. Disease, especially scurvy, caused many deaths, and it was not unusual for a ship to lose half its crew in a single voyage. While these discomforts made life unpleasant for the crew, the captain also had his difficulties. One of these was the constant fear of a mutiny, for the sailors of the time were rough and held life cheap, so that often the strongest discipline failed to keep them under control. Another of the captain's difficulties was a lack of charts and instruments to help him find his position. Thus the early Portuguese explorers were forced to keep within sight of the coast. By the end of the fifteenth century, however, a captain could keep track of his position reasonably well even when out of sight of land, for by then he had a compass and the means of calculating his latitude, and charts on which he could plot it. Vasco da Gama, for example, in 1497 remained out of sight of land from 3 August until 7 November and still knew where he was.

Despite the opinion of other people, and the obvious difficulties, Prince Henry remained firm in his determination to explore the African coast. Although he never went exploring himself, from his headquarters on the remote and rocky headland of Cape St Vincent he financed and encouraged exploration by others. Year after year his sea-captains would sail southwards from Portugal into the Atlantic and return—or not return—with news of what they had found. The first aim was to pass the supposed limit of navigation, Cape Bojador. Early explorers he employed thought this was impossible, and contented themselves with the discovery and exploration of Madeira and other of the Atlantic islands. But in 1434 one of Prince Henry's captains, Gil Eannes, successfully rounded the Cape and ended the belief that it was the limit of navigation. From that time the speed of exploration increased rapidly.

In 1441 the first Negroes were brought back to Portugal. Prince Henry had looked forward to this in the hope of converting them to Christianity. Some Portuguese merchants, however, looked upon the capture of the Negroes in a different way. To them it seemed a way of making a large profit by selling the Negroes as slaves to work on Portuguese farms where labour was scarce. Thus, Prince Henry's high hopes of converting the Negroes to Christianity degenerated into the beginnings of the European slave trade with Africa.

In 1443 the first gold-dust was obtained, but only as yet in very small quantities. Also, as exploration reached the coast beyond Sierra Leone it began to turn south-east and hopes were raised that it might continue directly to India and the eastern spice trade. Therefore, with the hope of reaching the spice markets of the Indian Ocean as well as the gold of West Africa, Portuguese exploration of the African coast continued even after Prince Henry's death in 1460. By 1475 they had found evidence of abundant gold in the Gold Coast region, and they had also found that the coast began to turn south-wards. This southward turn dismayed those who had hoped for a quick short route to the Indian Ocean, but exploration was not given up. In voyages made in 1482 and 1485 Diego Cam reached the mouth of the Congo and beyond, but more important was the expedition of Bartholomew Diaz who, in 1487, was blown round the Cape by a storm and found himself in the Indian Ocean. He sailed northwards as far as the Great Fish River, but at that point his men mutinied and forced him to return. It is said that Diaz named the Cape the 'Cape of Storms', and well he might for the great green rollers which sweep round the southern coast of Africa must have tossed the sturdy little Portuguese craft about like shells. It is said that the Portuguese king, full of hope at reaching the ocean where the eastern markets lay, renamed it the Cape of Good Hope. Meanwhile another Portuguese explorer, Covilham, had gone to Egypt and

India, and then had sailed in an Arab dhow southwards along the East African coast to Sofala.

The route to India was finally completed by an expedition which left Portugal in 1497. Its leader, Vasco da Gama, was able, brave and ruthless. When his men threatened to mutiny while rounding the Cape and demanded that the expedition should return to Portugal immediately, da Gama called them to a meeting on deck. Thinking that he was about to do as they wished the crew assembled. Then, in front of them all, da Gama took up the sailing charts of the Atlantic, threw them into the sea, and then told the men that the only man on board who could now take the ship back was himself and that he was going on. It was a bold action but it worked, and the voyage continued. By November he was in the Indian Ocean, and early in 1498 he reached the settlements of the Zenj empire. Then, having sailed northwards to Malindi, he turned eastwards to the market of Calicut on the west coast of India, where he collected a cargo of spices before returning to Portugal. The sea route to the East was open.

PORTUGUESE SETTLEMENTS

The Portuguese did not take an equal interest in all parts of the African coast. South Africa, for example, interested them hardly at all. They saw the Hottentot people there, and distributed copper coins and tin rings among them, but perhaps because the Hottentots could produce no trading item which interested them and often attacked their landing parties, the Portuguese generally left the southern coastline alone.

West Africa

West Africa, on the other hand, had been greatly valued from the beginning for its trade. Portuguese settlements there consisted of trading posts at those parts of the coast which provided the most valuable commodities and the most favourable places at which to anchor ships. The region from the Senegal to south of the Gambia was considered important for the rivers provided routes to the

27

interior, and the Cape Verde islands just off the coast were colonised by the Portuguese and formed good bases. The main trading items here were gold-dust, pepper and slaves, for which the Portuguese gave the coastal people cloth and metal goods. West of this region the coast provided few safe anchorages and so it was avoided until the Gold Coast region was reached. The Gold Coast itself was the greatest trading centre of all for it produced about 10 % of the world's gold supply in the early sixteenth century. To guard this valuable trade the Portuguese built fortresses at their main collecting bases, the chief of which was Elmina. Around these bases settlements of Negro traders from inland developed for the Portuguese were never allowed to gain control for themselves of the inland regions where the gold was mined. Further eastwards along the Guinea coast, the Niger Delta was valued by the Portuguese because they could obtain slaves from the Negro chiefs there and exchange them in the Gold Coast for gold. No permanent settlements were made on the delta as it was so unhealthy. Settlements were made, however, on the islands of São Thomé and Fernando Po which became important sugar-growing centres in the early sixteenth century.

Henry the Navigator had hoped to convert the people of West Africa as well as trading with them, and despite all their obvious failings the Portuguese did hope that their trading centres might also be missionary bases from which Christianity and European ways might spread inland. This did not happen. Instead, the Portuguese traders and commanders in West Africa tended to marry African wives until their settlements were half African and half European in their population and in their way of life. Inland the Negro people kept their tribal culture which was hardly influenced by the Portuguese at all.

The Congo and Angola

In the region of the Congo and Angola the Portuguese made some of their most interesting experiments in colonisation and missionary work. We have seen already that the King of Kongo was a powerful Bantu ruler with a large kingdom. From the start he was friendly to the Portuguese. In 1491 an expedition visited him at his capital, and he and his wife agreed to become Christians. The Portuguese were delighted. Priests were sent to Kongo to spread Christianity and the first Portuguese bishop to visit the capital had the 150 miles of his route from the coast covered by mats to show respect. Some Kongo people, including the king's son, were sent to Portugal to be taught the Christian faith. The king's son himself was made the first African bishop. Besides converting the Kongo people the Portuguese also tried to turn the capital into a city like those in Portugal. Therefore they named it San Salvador and sent hundreds of tons of stones in order to build magnificent churches and palaces there.

In the middle of the sixteenth century two misfortunes occurred. The first was a civil war, which was partly due to the changes which had been made, and this checked the spread of Portuguese influence although it did not stop it. The second misfortune was the invasion of Kongo by the warlike Jagga, who drove the king from his capital and forced him to flee to an island in the river. With Portuguese help the Jagga were driven out again, but the story of Kongo in the second half of the sixteenth century is a story of decline.

South of Kongo was Angola. The chief of this region, who was a subject of the King of Kongo, appealed for help to the Portuguese in 1574. As a result an expedition was sent to Angola led by Paulo Diaz, a grandson of the explorer who first rounded the Cape. Diaz gave the help required, and in 1576 he built a city on the mainland which became Loanda. He was pleased to notice that some of the Angola people were Christian, who had been converted by the Portuguese missionaries in Kongo. At first the relations between the Portuguese and Angola people were peaceful, but then the chief became afraid that the Portuguese might take his country, so he killed 500 of their soldiers whom he had asked to help him in a local war. Diaz at once attacked him, and in the fighting which followed the Portuguese gained control of the River Kwanza and the coast to the south where later Benguela was founded (1617). Angola, like the Guinea coast, became important for its export of slaves, most of whom were sent to Brazil where the Portuguese were developing sugar plantations, and which lay conveniently due west across the Atlantic from Angola. It is strange to remember that as the slaves were exported the Portuguese arranged that a bishop should bless them from his marble seat, which was specially built for the purpose upon the harbour side.

East Africa

Although the Portuguese passed by the region of the Cape of Good Hope they were very interested in the Arab settlements along the eastern coastline. There were two main reasons for their interest in this area.

The first was their desire to safeguard the route to India by gaining complete naval control of the Indian Ocean. Like all Europeans of the time the Portuguese believed that in order to make a good profit from trade in any commodity it was necessary to get rid of all competitors. Therefore, when Vasco da Gama reached the spice trade of the Indian Ocean he never thought of sharing that trade with the Arabs who then controlled it; instead the Portuguese determined to monopolise it and exclude the Arabs completely. They did this remarkably quickly because their navy was far stronger than any fleet of the Arabs. The capital of the trading empire they built up in the east was Goa, on the west coast of India, but their trading posts stretched to the East Indies themselves where the spices were actually grown. Goa was captured by the Portuguese in 1510. Within a few years of this date almost the whole trade from the east to Europe was in their hands. The East African coast was a vital part of their route.

The second reason why the Portuguese were interested in the east coast of Africa was because they hoped to benefit from the gold which was exported through Sofala.

Therefore, after a series of expeditions, the chief ones being those of 1505 and 1507, the Portuguese forced all the Arab settlements to accept their authority and pay them a yearly tribute. These settlements stretched from Barawa in the north southwards beyond Sofala, and included the islands of Mafia, Pemba and Zanzibar.

The headquarters of the Portuguese on the east coast became Mozambique. The Portuguese also settled at Sofala and at Kilwa, and in these places fortresses, churches and hospitals were built so that they became more and more like Portuguese towns and less and less like Arab ones. As ports of call for Portuguese ships these settlements were useful, but their trade was disappointing. One reason for the decline in trade was that the Portuguese settlements cut the Arab caravan trade inland, and it had been the caravans which had brought the valuable trading items to the coast. When they stopped, the gold export through Sofala, to take but one example, fell to 1 % of what it had been. In order to increase the output the Portuguese established trading posts about 100 miles up the Zambezi. In 1571–2 they also made an expedition with 1000 men up the river valley towards Monomotapa's kingdom, in the hope of gaining control of the source of the gold, but they were unsuccessful.

The Portuguese did not change the northern settlements as much as the southern ones. In the north the Portuguese generally left the Sultan of each settlement to rule as before, provided that the yearly tribute was paid. In the north, as in the south, trade inland was officially restricted, but in the north it was simpler to evade these restrictions because Portuguese ships and officials were fewer. Nevertheless the north also suffered a decline in prosperity. The great northern ally of the Portuguese was Malindi. From the very first arrival of da Gama in 1498 Malindi had been friendly, and that friendship remained throughout the period of Portuguese control. But Mombasa, which was the largest of all the east coast settlements in 1500, was very different. From the first Mombasa had been hostile to the Portuguese and it remained the great trouble centre for 200 years. Its name, which means 'The Island of War', was most suitable during this time. At the end of the sixteenth century the Portuguese decided that Mombasa should be made into a fortified centre to control their northern possessions on the coast, and in 1593 they started to build Fort Jesus and introduced a Portuguese garrison and settlers. But Mombasa remained defiant. It had rebelled before and it was to rebel again.

The northern and southern settlements of the Portuguese remained almost entirely coastal and they affected the African people very little. Even the Christian missions which they started had no permanent effect upon the tribes of the mainland. As the Portuguese affected them so little the African people on the mainland generally left them in peace. Gold and ivory were obtained from chiefs for cloth and beads, and African slaves were obtained for labour at the coast. There was also some intermarriage as very few Portuguese women came to Africa. Otherwise there was very little contact and the African people went on as before.

CHAPTER 4

THE LOST CENTURIES (1600–1800)

EUROPEAN INTEREST IN AFRICA BEFORE 1600

Until the start of the seventeenth century the Portuguese possessions in Africa were not seriously threatened by any other European country.

This does not mean, however, that none of the other European countries showed any interest in Portuguese exploration and settlement. They did. From the beginning the voyages and cargoes of the Portuguese explorers had been watched with great curiosity. In the fifteenth century Castile, which later combined with Aragon to form the kingdom of Spain, had followed the Portuguese along the coast and rivalled them for possession of the Atlantic islands. Castile and Portugal might also have become serious rivals for settlement on the African coast, had it not been for Columbus' discovery of the New World on behalf of Castile in 1492, and the Treaty of Tordesillas (1494) which recognised Portugal's right to exploration to the East (Africa and Asia) and Castile's right to exploration to the West (the West Indies and the Americas). From that time Castile and Spain concentrated on the development of their own western possessions, and their rivalry with the Portuguese in Africa virtually ceased.

In the sixteenth century the French and English began to make voyages to West Africa. They hoped to make a profit from getting gold, pepper and slaves, but their voyages were not regular or large and the loss of human life as a result of disease was frightening. An English voyage in 1553 started with 140 men and came back with only 40 still alive. The Portuguese protested that these voyages were illegal and some attempt was made to patrol the coast, but on the whole the interference was very small, and throughout the century the Portuguese remained the only European settlers on the coast and easily the most important traders there.

THE ATLANTIC TRADE AND WEST AFRICA

But in the seventeenth century the position changed. One of the reasons for this was the decline of Portuguese power, which had been evident long before the seventeenth century began. Their population was too small to hold their widespread possessions in the East Indies, India, Africa and Brazil; their navy had become inefficient, and their annexation by Spain in 1580 had involved them in hostilities with the enemies of Spain. The chief of these enemies were the Dutch and the English, who had both fought for their existence against the power of Spain, and who both possessed strong navies and wanted to increase their strength and prosperity by developing overseas trade.

It was the Dutch who made the first and fiercest attack. In 1602 they started the Dutch East India Company. By 1610 they had made themselves the strongest power in the Indian Ocean, and had taken control of the spice trade with the East from the Portuguese. Meanwhile, the English, on a smaller scale, also formed an East India Company which forced the Portuguese to share their trade to India.

The Dutch were not content with the control of the eastern trade. They also wanted to control the trade of the Atlantic, and for this reason in 1621 they started the Dutch West India Company.

As the Atlantic trade had important results for Africa we must look

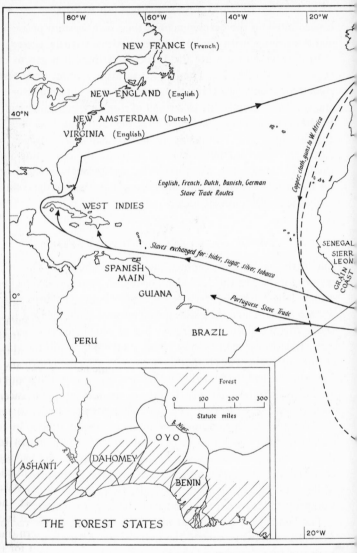

Map 4. Slaving and other trade routes

34

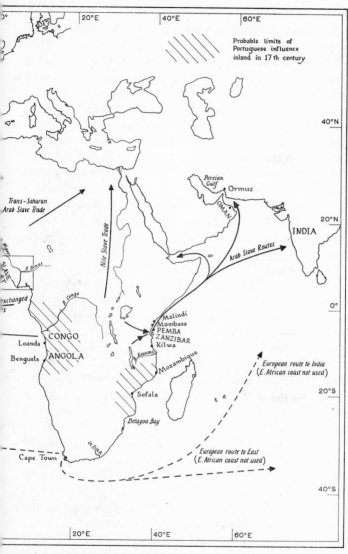

Probable limits of
Portuguese influence
inland in 17th century

40°N

Persian
Gulf
Ormuz

OMAN

20°N

INDIA

Trans-Saharan
Arab Slave Trade

Nile Slave Trade

Arab Slave Routes

R. Benue

Niger
SLAVE

R. Congo

0°

exchanged
s

CONGO

Malindi
Mombasa
PEMBA
ZANZIBAR
Kilwa

Loanda

Benguela   ANGOLA

R. Rovuma

Mozambique

European route to India
(E. African coast not used)

Sofala

20°S

Delagoa Bay

R. Limpopo

Cape Town

European route to East
(E. African coast not used)

40°S

20°E   40°E   60°E

seventeenth and eighteenth centuries.

35

at it more closely. Until the fifteenth century the Mediterranean had been the most important seaway for trade in the western world. From its eastern end the valuable goods from Asia had been carried to Venice and Genoa, the great seaports of Europe. But when America was discovered in the west, and the Portuguese succeeded in getting all the way to the east by sea, the Atlantic Ocean—which led to the east via the Cape and to America by sailing west—became increasingly important. At first the eastern trade via the Cape was easily the more important, but as settlement in America and the West Indies developed the trade to the west increased in value. The great demand of the Spanish who were the first colonists was for labour—labour for the extremely valuable silver mines in Mexico, labour for the ranches, and labour for the lowland plantations. On an unlucky day for Africa the idea of getting slave labour from West Africa was suggested. It proved popular because the Negroes were strong and used to working in a hot climate, and because transport across the Atlantic was a fairly simple process. At first the Spanish gave the Portuguese a monopoly (called the 'Asiento') of the carrying and selling of slaves across the Atlantic, and during the sixteenth century they were the main suppliers. But in the seventeenth century the English, French and Dutch became interested in colonising the New World, and by the middle of the century the colonies included practically the whole Atlantic coastline of North America and the main West Indian islands. Moreover, the discovery was made that on these islands sugar cane could be grown on plantations from which tremendous profits resulted when the sugar was sold in Europe. So the trade with the New World became as much worth fighting for as the trade with the East, and one of the vital parts of that trade was the supply of slaves from West Africa on which the West Indies especially were entirely dependent. From the middle of the seventeenth century, when large-scale sugar plantations became popular in the West Indies, the slave trade became a big concern.

Such was the Atlantic trade which the Dutch West India Company wanted to control. The efficiency and strength of their shipping made them successful. They attacked Spanish shipping, they temporarily captured Brazil from the Portuguese, and they carried goods across the Atlantic for the French and English colonies as well. But the most profitable trade was that of carrying slaves from West Africa because the demand for them was always greater than the number which could be supplied. Therefore the Dutch West India Company set out to take this trade from the Portuguese, and by 1642 all the Portuguese possessions on the Gold Coast, and some elsewhere, had been captured.

French and English rivalry for the Atlantic trade

The Dutch control of the Atlantic trade was soon challenged by the English and French, who, from 1650, forbade the Dutch to carry goods to or from their colonies. This meant that the French and English themselves would have to provide their colonies with slaves, and this meant gaining positions in West Africa. The Dutch tried to keep them out but they failed, and during the second half of the seventeenth century the English and French—as well as Swedes, Danes and Germans (Brandenburgers)—gained possessions on the West Coast where they collected slaves and traded. By the end of the seventeenth century the Dutch were no longer the greatest power in the Atlantic trade. Instead, during the eighteenth century, the two great rival European countries concerned with American colonies and trade were Britain and France. After a series of wars, the French agreed in the Treaty of Paris (1763) to give up their colonies in North America although not in the West Indies. Britain gained what France had lost, and became easily the greatest naval power and easily the greatest colonising power in North America. From West Africa's point of view this meant that Britain became the greatest carrier of slaves across the Atlantic, with France second and with the Dutch and Danes carrying a few as well. Meanwhile, the Portuguese maintained a steady export of slaves across the Atlantic from their colony of Angola to their colony of Brazil. In volume the Portuguese slave trade compared with that of the French.

37

The Atlantic slave trade

How did the Atlantic slave trade work? From the point of view of the West African chiefs the facts were simple and attractive. Europeans would exchange copper and iron bars, cloth, guns and other valuable items for slaves. Slaves could easily be obtained by tribal warfare, and sometimes by punishing wrongdoers of one's own tribe. The more slaves a chief could provide the more items could he get to make himself rich and strong. So slaves were obtained in ever-increasing numbers. From the point of view of the European slave traders the facts were also attractive. Their trade was triangular. They exchanged their exports on the West African coast for slaves and made a profit there; they sailed across the Atlantic and exchanged the slaves for hides, silver and sugar, making a profit again; then they returned to Europe and sold the hides, silver and sugar for far more than their original exports had cost. From the point of view of the colonists in the West Indies and America the slave trade seemed a necessity. There seemed no other possible source of labour, and without labour their plantations, which made them some of the richest men in the world, could not continue. For political reasons also the trade was desirable. The European countries which took part became wealthier because of their plantations, and they became stronger at sea because of the number of ships that were built to carry the slaves. Thus, there were strong reasons why the slave trade flourished despite the terrible suffering it caused.

Accurate figures are impossible to give, but guesses have been made that about one million slaves were exported across the Atlantic in the sixteenth century, three million in the seventeenth century, and seven million in the eighteenth century.

Although the whole of the West African coast was affected, most slaves were taken from east of the Gold Coast. The French concentrated first on the Senegal region where they established trading bases, and then on the Slave Coast region. The British, like the Dutch and the Danes, concentrated first on the Gold Coast and then extended their interests eastwards. The main Portuguese interests were in the Congo and Angola but they were also active in Guinea, the Gold Coast, the Slave Coast and the Oil Rivers. Sometimes these countries organised Companies to control the trade, and on the Gold Coast and elsewhere forts were built by the Companies to make their position safe. But most of the trade seems to have been carried on by individual traders, who hoped to make one or two voyages and thus become rich for the rest of their lives.

THE RESULTS OF THE SLAVE TRADE:
THE FOREST STATES

What were the effects of the Atlantic slave trade on West Africa? Most trade helps the progress of a country by bringing ideas, and wealth and a higher standard of living. If the European countries had been interested only in pepper, ivory and gold this would probably have been true in West Africa. But unfortunately the chief interest was in slaves, and the slave trade did not encourage progress. In fact it encouraged disorder because tribes fought one another for slaves. This must also have had some effect by decreasing the population, but this was probably only a very small proportion of the total because the areas which were most affected are among the most densely populated in West Africa today.

The slave trade also had a considerable effect on the development of African states in the forest area of Guinea. At first it seemed to encourage their growth because the guns and the wealth which they obtained by trading with the Europeans made them strong. But as they depended for their wealth upon slaves captured in war they became corrupt and unpopular. At first the slave trade helped them to flourish, but in the long run it ruined them. Yet it is worth remembering that although these states depended so much upon the slave trade, and although the most horrible cruelties were common, these people were also skilled in some of the arts of peace and produced excellent models in bronze and brass.

Oyo

The four main states which developed during this period were

39

Oyo, Benin, Dahomey and Ashanti. The first and greatest of these was Oyo. The Yoruba people who now live in this part of Nigeria have many traditions and stories about their early chiefs—one of them, Sango, was said to have been so fierce that fire came from his mouth and smoke from his nose—but exact dates and facts are lacking. Perhaps the origin of Oyo lies in the movement of people from the north-west around A.D. 1000 or before. Certainly by the eighteenth century the state was at its strongest and largest, and included much more than the modern province of Oyo. With the chief purpose of obtaining slaves for sale to European traders its rulers began to attack the regions around them and as each new area was conquered it was occupied. So Oyo became rich, or rather the chief and his friends did. Meanwhile the smaller chiefs and the conquered areas became jealous, and in the early nineteenth century they rebelled and the Oyo empire broke up. In the north the Muslim Fulani emirs became the rulers, and in the south the chiefs fought one another in a long series of wars. Slaving went on throughout this period although the European demand for slaves had stopped.

Benin

The people of Benin were influenced by Oyo although they did not come under its rule. The Portuguese had visited Benin as early as 1485 and it developed as an important trading centre between the Yoruba people and European traders. By the middle of the seventeenth century Benin had extended its rule from Lagos in the west to Bonny in the east. Then came decline. The wars for slaving left the country weak and underpopulated until the once great city of Benin itself began to fall to pieces through poverty and neglect, although again the horrors of slaving and human sacrifice went on.

Dahomey

To the west of Benin lay the little coastal states of Whydah and Jacquin. These grew in importance with the slave trade. But north of them, inland, another state was developing. This was Dahomey.

40

The rulers of Dahomey wanted to deal directly with the European slavers, and so in the 1720's they conquered the coastal states. Although hostilities occurred with the Oyo people in the east and with the Ashanti people in the west Dahomey managed to hold what it had gained until her relations with the European powers on the coast became hostile.

Ashanti

In the Middle Ages groups of Akan-speaking peoples, with immigrants from the Sudan, formed several separate states in the forest north of the Gold Coast. Each of these states had a ruler whose position was shown by a stool or throne. These states made alliances with one another during the seventeenth century, and at the end of it the Kumasi chief, Osei Tutu, formed these small territories into a really strong nation known as the Ashanti Union. According to tradition Osei Tutu achieved this by calling all the states to a meeting at which a golden stool descended in a cloud of dust upon him, while thunder and darkness made the scene still more impressive. As a result the rulers who occupied the Golden Stool of the state of Kumasi were recognised as the head of all the Ashanti nation and a tremendous feeling of unity was achieved. In the century that followed, to increase their wealth, they became slavers on a huge scale conquering northwards and southwards, until by 1800 they came into contact with the Fante people and Europeans on the coast. Hostilities with these eventually led to the defeat of the Ashanti.

Besides influencing the development of these forest states, the slave trade also had the effect of permanently increasing the contacts between Europe and West Africa. Although at first the contacts were only through Companies and individual traders, after the Treaty of Paris (1763) the British government officially constituted all the captured French possessions in Upper Gambia (except Goree which became French again) and their own posts in that area into the crown colony of Senegambia. As we shall see, this official government control was extended in the nineteenth century to all the other regions of British trading interests in West Africa.

While European connexions with West Africa increased as a result of the slave trade, in another part of Africa a European settlement was started for quite different reasons, and this became the largest of all European settlements in the whole African continent. It was started at the Cape of Good Hope and the people who started it were the Dutch.

We have already seen that at the very beginning of the seventeenth century the Dutch successfully fought the Portuguese for their trade with the East. They founded their East India Company to control the trade they had won, and this Company established the first settlement at Table Bay in 1652 as a supply base for their ships on the six months' voyage to the Indies. This remained its chief purpose until the opening of the Suez Canal (1869), and the number of ships calling each year at Table Bay increased steadily. At first they were nearly all Dutch, but by 1780 more than half were English or French as their interests in India and the East became important.

Dutch settlement at the Cape did not grow rapidly. The first settlers of 1652, led by the weather-beaten little Dutch surgeon Van Riebeeck, were all Company officials. In 1657 other settlers were also admitted. They grew wheat and tobacco, and they began cattle trading with the Hottentots. They also began to dislike the strict monopoly and control which was enforced by the Company. The Dutch were not the only settlers. Germans also came and so did French Protestants (called Huguenots) when Louis XIV, in 1685, withdrew the Edict of Nantes which had granted them toleration. They became valuable farmers, especially in connexion with wine production.

During the eighteenth century settlement in South Africa developed in a way of its own. Cape Town remained the administrative centre where the Governor and his Council of Policy resided. By

1780 it contained about 1000 houses all neatly whitewashed and prettily shaped. Around Cape Town were the wheat and wine producers. But most typical were the stock farmers of the interior who had obtained large grants of land for their cattle and lived simple, isolated lives rarely visiting Cape Town except perhaps for the annual Communion or to get a marriage licence. The isolated conditions in which these cattle-farmers lived led to the development of a special language which later became known as 'Afrikaans', while the people themselves became known as 'Afrikaners' (Africans) or 'Boers' (farmers).

In the Cape, as elsewhere, colonisation needed labour. Very early in the colony's history the question arose as to whether this should be supplied by slaves. In 1717 the decision was made that it should. From that time the number of slaves increased to considerable proportions. They were used in homes and on farms, and they came from several sources. Some were local Hottentots, some were from East and West Africa, and some came from Malay. A good deal of mixing took place between these racial groups and a few of the whites and the Cape Coloured people of today are their descendants. The treatment of these slaves was no worse than elsewhere— probably it was better—but the idea grew in the minds of the Afrikaners that between themselves and other races God had made an unbridgeable gap. As they were sincerely and fiercely religious this idea had a deep and lasting importance.

Until the latter part of the eighteenth century the only African people with whom the Cape settlers came in contact were the Bush-men and Hottentots. In the early years the Hottentots made some attempts to expel the Dutch, but finding that such attempts were useless they gave them up. The Dutch meanwhile became interested in buying their cattle and using their labour. By 1713 most of the cattle had been sold, many of the people had died of smallpox, and the Hottentots as an organised people were finished. The Bushmen were even more unfortunate than the Hottentots. As hunters, the Bushmen opposed all settlement and again and again they raided and attacked the European intruders. As a result the settlers' attitude towards them was one of merciless hostility, and fighting parties called 'Commandos' were organised to chase and kill all Bushmen raiders. But a much more serious power than either the Hottentots or Bushmen was that of the Bantu tribes who were expanding south-wards from Central Africa at the same time as the European settlers were expanding northwards from the Cape. They met approximately at the line running westwards from the Great Fish River in the later years of the eighteenth century. The Afrikaners called the Bantu people 'Kaffirs' ('unbelievers') and from 1781 a series of 'Kaffir Wars' began as the Bantu and Europeans fought each other for land. In the early nineteenth century this struggle became the chief factor in South Africa's history.

THE CONGO, ANGOLA AND EAST AFRICA

We have seen that because the Portuguese had become so weak they lost their possessions on the Guinea coast. How much else did they lose?

The Congo and Angola

In the regions of the Congo and Angola the Portuguese had to struggle against the Dutch, who took Loanda, from 1640 to 1648, and against attacks from the African people. Their main African opponent was a lady called Jinga. Having poisoned her brother in order to become Queen she started a rebellion in 1621 against the Portuguese. It lasted for thirty years, but the Portuguese held on, and Angola became increasingly important because it supplied the main Portuguese colony of Brazil with slaves. But the seventeenth and eighteenth centuries were generally a time of muddle so far as this area was concerned. Governors came and went after very short periods; agriculture was so little developed that the Portuguese were hardly self-supporting; missionary activity had occasional bursts of life but in 1800 all missions were withdrawn from the kingdom of Kongo though not from Angola. Some attempts were made to explore inland and a number of forts were established, but although

44

Portuguese authority was theoretically recognised as far north as
Ambriz it had very little effect outside Loanda and Benguela.

East Africa

On the east coast the chief opponents of the Portuguese were the
Arabs, not the Dutch. The Dutch did make a few attempts to take
Mozambique, but as the main trade route to the East had changed
to the east of Madagascar, the East African coast had ceased to play
an important part in European trade. But although Europeans were
not particularly interested in taking the Portuguese possessions in
this area the Arabs were. They heard that the Dutch had defeated
the Portuguese in the Indies; they heard that the English had
defeated them off the coast of India, and in 1622 they heard that the
Persians had driven the Portuguese from Ormuz. As usual Mombasa
was the first of the East African towns to attempt rebellion. After a
short-lived rising in 1631, Mombasa was finally taken from the
Portuguese in 1698 after one of the most horrible sieges in history.
It lasted thirty-three months, and of the 2500 people who had
entered Fort Jesus at the start, only thirteen of those who remained
were alive at the end. The conquerer, Sultan bin Seif, was the
Imam of Oman on the Persian Gulf. After capturing Mombasa in
1699, he also drove the Portuguese from Pemba and Kilwa. Then
he had to return to his kingdom of Oman, leaving Omani Arabs to
rule his East African conquests on his behalf. In Mombasa he left
the Mazrui family.

The conquests of Sultan bin Seif ended Portuguese power in the
north. They had been very unpopular rulers, and apart from intro-
ducing a few crops, including maize, they had made very little
difference to East Africa despite their influence during two centuries.
They had, however, succeeded in destroying the wealth of the Arab
settlements and in the eighteenth century these settlements struggled
without success to regain their former prosperity. They also continued their rivalry with one another, but never to the extent of
letting the Portuguese recapture them.

To the south, from the Rovuma River to Delagoa Bay, the Portuguese remained in control of the coast. During the first half of the seventeenth century their influence and wealth in this region increased. One reason was the decline of the power of Muene Motapa, who accepted Portuguese protection over his kingdom in 1629. Another reason was the development of an export of slaves which brought a considerable profit for a time, although it also caused other types of trade to decrease. But the story of the Portuguese in this region during the seventeenth and eighteenth centuries is generally one of decline and corruption. The African people were disturbed by the monopoly trading companies of the Portuguese, and by the Dominican and Jesuit missionaries, so that during the early eighteenth century there were several African revolts. Meanwhile the Portuguese traders, by taking for themselves the profits which were supposed to go to their Companies, often lived in oriental luxury surrounded by slaves and concubines. Attempts to improve the trading and administrative arrangements were made from time to time, but corruption was too deep and the attempts failed.

At first the government of Portuguese East Africa had been supervised from Goa, but in 1752 it became separate. The East African possessions were divided into five captaincies which were supervised by a Captain-General who lived at Mozambique. Mozambique was the capital and in 1807 its population included 500 Europeans, most of whom were transported criminals or half-castes, 6000 slaves, and about 250 Indian traders known as banyans. According to a Portuguese description of 1785 the settlements were in such a state of decay that industry and trade had practically ceased.

CONCLUSION

We have called the period from 1600 to 1800 'The Lost Centuries' because the outside contacts with Europe brought more harm than good to Africa. Fortunately the centuries which followed were to prove more valuable.

PART III

THE EUROPEAN PENETRATION OF THE INTERIOR

INTRODUCTION

A rope is made from many parts, or strands, which are wound together. So was Africa's history in the nineteenth century. That too was made up of many interwoven strands which produced the main story of the spread of European influence from the coast to the interior. In this chapter we shall look at some of those strands, and especially those which affected the whole continent.

THE ABOLITION OF THE SLAVE TRADE

One of the big changes which took place in the early nineteenth century was the attitude of European countries towards the African slave trade. For hundreds of years this had been considered so valuable and necessary that it had been the main reason for European interest in Africa. But in the nineteenth century it was abolished.

The first European country which effectively forbade her subjects to continue the trade was Denmark in 1804, but this did not make much difference to the number of slaves who were exported because Denmark was a small country with a small navy. It was much more important when Britain, which had the largest navy in the world and was the chief carrier of the Atlantic slave trade, forbade her subjects from continuing in 1808. The Act which made the slave trade illegal for British people was the result of the efforts of a small group of men led by William Wilberforce. First they had to make people realise the misery which the trade involved, for very few people knew anything about it, and then they had to get Parliament to stop it officially. That was where Wilberforce was so useful. He was very rich and very talented—he was clever, popular, and had a superb voice. He was always being asked to parties, and if he had wished he could have spent his whole life on pleasure alone and done no work at all. But in 1785 he became convinced that it was his duty to lead the demand in Parliament to abolish the slave trade, and he gave up all his time to achieving this. There were many people who objected. The slave traders themselves of course opposed his demands, and so did the West Indian planters who feared they would be ruined if the slave supply was ended. Many government officials also opposed the abolition of the trade because they thought the West Indies were the most profitable part of the Empire. Many of the leaders of the navy, including Lord Nelson, opposed Wilberforce too because they believed that fewer ships might be built if the slave trade ended and that might mean that Britain would have fewer ships in case of war. In addition to this, from the 1790's until 1815, Britain was fighting for her existence against the French led by Napoleon, and most people were too worried about the war to take any interest in abolition. But, despite the people who shook their fists at him and the people who laughed at him, Wilberforce reminded Parliament year after year that the slave trade was wrong and should be abolished. At last the people of England and the members of Parliament were convinced, and the slave trade was made illegal by an act which was passed in 1807 and was enforced from 1808. From that time no British ships could carry slaves or take any part in the slave trade.

When the buying and selling of slaves had been made illegal in the British Empire, the next step was to abolish slavery as well by forbidding anyone to own a slave. This was not achieved until 1833, and it meant that Britain had to pay £20 million compensation to the slave owners who now had to free their slaves. Although Wilberforce died a month before the final passing of this bill he lived long enough to know that its passing was certain. 'Thank God,' he said, 'that I should witness a day in which England is willing to give £20 million for the abolition of slavery.'

These acts had very important results in West Africa and in South Africa, as we shall see, but they only affected British ships and areas administered or protected by Britain. They did not affect other European countries, some of whom took over the transport of slaves which Britain had given up, nor did they affect the Sultan of Zanzibar who ruled the east coast. But during the nineteenth century one by one the other countries also ceased to trade in slaves or to own them, and the way was open for peaceful trade and progress.

MISSIONARY SOCIETIES

Another strand in the opening of Africa was a renewed strong desire among Christians in Europe to convert and help the African people. We have seen how this motive encouraged Henry the Navigator in the fifteenth century, and how the Portuguese did set up missions in the coastal areas they controlled and especially in the kingdom of Kongo. But we have also seen that the desire to convert and help the African people was replaced by the still greater desire for slaves and the profits which came from them. That was a grim story. But it is encouraging to remember that in the late eighteenth century and early nineteenth century sincere attempts were made to put right the wrongs which had been done. In Britain, following a religious revival, the Protestant churches at last began to realise their responsibilities in missionary activity and several societies were started soon after one another—the Baptist Missionary Society began in 1792, the London Missionary Society in 1795, the Scottish Missionary Society in 1796, the Church Missionary Society in 1799, the British and Foreign Bible Society in 1804, and the Methodist Missionary Society in 1813. The Roman Catholic Church also made renewed and greater missionary efforts, and in 1868 the White Fathers were started for missionary work in Africa. This revival of missionary activity, which was directed towards many parts of the world, had extremely important results. Missionaries were anxious to reach new tribes and to end the slave trade, so they were among the chief explorers of the interior. They were sympathetic towards the African people so they vigorously and effectively opposed any exploitation by traders or settlers. They not only talked about the

49

Christian gospel; they were also the pioneers in starting hospitals and schools, and in spreading the valuable lessons of European civilisation. Many missionaries died from illness within a few weeks of their arrival; all made tremendous sacrifices, but the service they gave to Africa was of immense value.

TRADE

Trade has always been one of the greatest forces encouraging exploration and development, and when the slave trade ended other sorts of trade still continued. At the end of the eighteenth century Britain, and later other countries of Europe, developed the use of the steam engine for driving machinery, and great wealth began to come from the exports of the factories which developed. This change, known as the Industrial Revolution, caused a great increase in production and one result was that manufacturers and traders showed a special interest in Africa, partly as a supplier of raw materials, and even more as a market where their products could be sold. Often it was the trader who first penetrated into the interior and who became the chief influence over the area in which he traded.

GEOGRAPHY

A renewed interest in the geography of Africa also encouraged exploration. Exaggerated stories of rich cities in the Sudan were well known in Europe in the eighteenth century, and there were various guesses about lakes and mountains in the central part of Africa which map-makers sometimes included in their maps. The two main problems were to find the mouth of the Niger and the source of the Nile. In order to discover the Niger's course and mouth the Africa Association was started in Britain in 1788, and was later reorganised as the Royal Geographical Society in 1830. As we shall see, these societies encouraged and financed some of the most valuable explorations of the century.

POLITICS

Political motives also encouraged the penetration of Africa. Britain was the European country which played the leading part because in the nineteenth century it was the strongest and wealthiest country in Europe. British statesmen found Africa a problem. They wanted to end the slave trade, they wanted to get the profits of legitimate trade, and they wanted to control the Cape and keep on friendly terms with the Sultan of Zanzibar in order to guard their communications with India and the East. But they did not want to pay the expenses of defending and administering African territories. For most of the century British statesmen tried to have the benefits of their connexions with Africa while accepting the minimum of responsibility. Then, in most cases, they decided that compromise was impossible and they took over the regions with which they were connected and reluctantly paid the expense which this involved. Other European countries looked upon these British connexions with envy, and towards the end of the century claims were made to many African territories by various European powers, often with the main idea of getting wealth and power from them. In almost every case they were disappointed. In fact, it was Britain's wealth which enabled her to administer and develop her African possessions. It was not her African possessions which made her wealthy.

SCIENCE

Scientific developments in Europe also played their part in the penetration of Africa. They stopped the tremendous death rate from malaria by the discovery of quinine, and so made it possible for Europeans to live safely in the tropics. They brought East Africa thousands of miles nearer to Europe when the Suez Canal was opened in 1869. And, at the end of the century, the steam engine at last made it comparatively easy to reach the African interior by means of railways.

THE AFRICAN ATTITUDE TO EUROPEAN PENETRATION

How did the African people regard this penetration? Sometimes explorers, missionaries and traders were met by tribes who were hostile. More often they were met by curiosity and suspicion, for it was very strange indeed to see for the first time a man who was white instead of black. It was also very strange to see his clothes and his instruments. The Masai who met Bishop Hannington were amazed by his blue socks and thought he must be toeless; they were even more amazed by his watch whose tick they thought was made by a spirit inside. But it is unwise to generalise very far, for receptions differed from place to place. It would, however, be true to say that generally the African people welcomed the obvious benefits that the white man brought, such as medicine; they accepted his rule as inevitable because he had far better weapons than they had; but they came to dislike more and more the European claims to African land.

It is now time to see how the various strands worked together in each part of Africa.

CHAPTER 5

THE PENETRATION OF WEST AFRICA

THE ABOLITION OF THE SLAVE TRADE

The main strand in the history of West Africa during this period is the influence of the campaign to end the slave trade. The most obvious methods of doing this were by means of naval patrols, and by getting other European countries concerned to co-operate in the anti-slave trade movement. Such co-operation was not easy to obtain, and until slavery was abolished in the United States of America in 1863 large numbers of ships continued to carry slaves across the Atlantic. The naval patrols tried to catch them, but only a small proportion were caught.

In any case it was not only across the Atlantic that slaves were carried. African chiefs in Dahomey, Benin and elsewhere still went on slaving when the Atlantic trade had ended. In view of this, the leaders of the British abolition movement realised that if the slave trade was to end then something else must be put in its place and peace must be established. Therefore they encouraged legitimate trade, they encouraged exploration of the interior, and they encouraged the British government to increase its influence and administration in West Africa in order to obtain peace. The missionary societies agreed with the abolitionists and helped them, and in every region of West Africa missionaries were among the pioneers of development. Sometimes the missionaries were themselves Africans. One of the greatest missionaries to the Gold Coast was the Rev. Thomas Birch Freeman who worked in the Fante states from 1837 until 1890. He was the son of an African father and English mother. In Nigeria Samuel Crowther, a Yoruba, was consecrated as Bishop of the Niger in 1864.

SIERRA LEONE

Before the slave trade had been made illegal for British ships a new colony had been started in West Africa. This was Sierra Leone. Its aim was to provide a home for the Negro slaves who had been freed in England in 1772, and those who had been freed in America after the War of Independence in 1783. It was started by the abolitionists who organised the Sierra Leone Company. In 1787 they sent out a small group of Negro men and English women, but many died from disease and the rest became discontented when they realised that they would have to work in order to provide food for themselves. However, despite tremendous difficulties, the settlement survived and was officially taken over by the British government in 1808. Freetown, its capital, then became the base from which the British navy patrolled the coast to intercept slave ships. In 1822, on the coast nearby, the American Colonisation Society started similar settlements which became the colony of Liberia. In 1841 Liberia had its first Negro Governor, J. J. Roberts, and in 1847 it became a Republic and adopted a constitution similar to that of the United States. It did not, however, have much influence inland and its development was slow owing to lack of money.

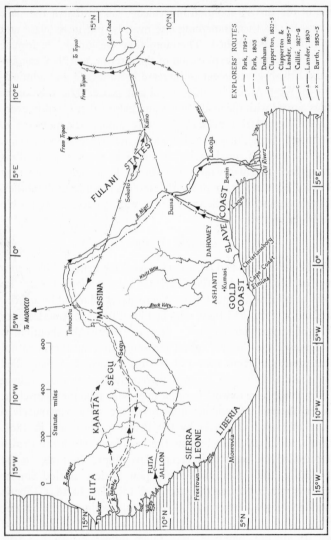

EXPLORERS' ROUTES

Park, 1795–7
Park, 1805
Denham &
Clapperton, 1822–5
Clapperton &
Lander, 1825–7
Caillié, 1827–8
Lander, 1830
Barth, 1850–5

Map 5. West Africa in the nineteenth century.

EXPLORATION

While these new colonies were starting, attempts were being made to explore the interior, and especially to explore the Niger. These attempts were made by the Africa Association. The first three were failures, but in 1795 a young Scottish doctor, Mungo Park, succeeded in making his way from the Gambia to Segu on the Niger. His efforts aroused great interest and ten years later he set off again intending to sail down the river to its mouth. He never got there. Instead, most of his thirty-nine companions died of fever, and with a few survivors he was last heard of continuing downstream in a canoe. Years later it was reported that he had been drowned at rapids near Bussa. Further expeditions to find the Niger's mouth were made by Denham and Clapperton (1822–5) and by Clapperton and Lander (1825–7). However, it was not until 1830, when Lander sailed downstream from Bussa to the sea, that it was realised that the mass of swamps, lagoons and streams, which Europeans had previously called the Oil Rivers, was actually the Niger delta. Other explorations in West Africa by Englishmen and Frenchmen can be seen on the map, but special mention must be made of the German, Dr Barth, who spent from 1850 to 1855 exploring the Sudan. His descriptions of what he saw gave Europeans their first accurate idea of this region.

THE GOLD COAST

While European explorers were visiting the interior, the British were becoming increasingly involved in affairs on the coast. When Sierra Leone was taken over by the government in 1808 there were only two other areas of British settlement on the west coast. They were Gambia and the Gold Coast, which were both supervised by the Company of Merchants which was dissolved in 1821. All three settlements (Sierra Leone, Gambia, the Gold Coast) then came under the control of the Governor of Sierra Leone who was Sir Charles Macarthy. This vigorous, well-intentioned Governor was quite sure that the best policy was to increase British influence inland in order to end the slave trade and keep the peace, but in 1824 he was killed while attempting to drive the Ashanti back from their raids on the Gold Coast, and his skull was kept as a magic weapon by the chiefs of Kumasi.

The British government then decided to withdraw from the Gold Coast, but trade was still continued with the region by a Committee of Merchants. In 1830 this committee sent a young officer, Captain George Maclean, to look after their trading interests there. He did this so effectively that he succeeded in making himself the chief influence in the region by giving protection to the Fante tribe on the coast, and by driving back the Ashanti. This increase of influence alarmed the British government in England because they feared that it would involve them in increased expense. The missionary societies were also alarmed because they suspected—quite wrongly—that Maclean was secretly allowing the slave trade to continue and exploiting the African people. Suspicions grew still more serious when Maclean married a well-known lady in 1838 and she was found dead as a result of poisoning a year later. It was not until a Parliamentary commission made a full report that Maclean was completely cleared of all the suspicions against him and praised for the work he had done. He continued to work on the Gold Coast until 1847.

Meanwhile, as a result of the Commission's report, the British government in 1843 again took over official responsibility for the Gold Coast forts which were again placed under the supervision of the Governor of Sierra Leone until 1850. In addition to taking over the forts the British officials also made agreements, or 'Bonds', with the coastal tribes by which they agreed to end some of their more savage customs such as human sacrifice. These 'bonds' did not give the British any authority over the government of the tribes with whom they were made. However, the African states concerned were often called a British Protectorate, and, as we shall see, the agreements did have the effect of involving the British in wars against the Ashanti when they invaded.

THE OIL RIVERS AREA AND THE NIGER EXPEDITIONS

What was happening to the east of the Gold Coast? Here, in the regions of the Slave Coast and the Oil Rivers, the fierce kings of Dahomey and Benin still continued slaving on a great scale. In an attempt to reduce the slave export from the coast the British captured Lagos in 1851 and annexed it as a colony ten years later. This reduced the trade, but it certainly did not stop it. While slaving still went on through the African chiefs, Europeans were interested in this part of the coast for legitimate trading purposes. The main item was palm oil and the Oil Rivers were so called because they were the main area from which this oil was obtained. It was useful for lubricating machinery, for making soap and for making candles, and several trading companies had been formed to carry on the oil trade. Their methods were often as rough and unscrupulous as those of the slave trade had been.

These oil companies kept to the coastal area. The first attempts to trade inland were made by a group of people who were chiefly interested in ending slaving in the interior by encouraging peaceful trade and development there. They were organised by Macgregor Laird who arranged a series of steamboat expeditions up the Niger because this seemed to offer the best route inland. The first expedition sailed in 1832 and the next in 1841. Both were terrible failures mainly because so many people died from disease. But in 1854 another expedition did succeed in sailing up the Niger without loss of life, owing to the discovery that quinine prevented malaria. This discovery made trade inland possible. Dr Baikie, the leader of the 1854 expedition, became the British consul at Lokoja, and in the next ten years several trading stations were started on the river.

THE GOLD COAST AND ASHANTI WARS

Meanwhile affairs on the Gold Coast were unsettled. The rapidly changing British officials had not won the respect of the coastal people as Maclean had done, and the Ashantis were a permanent threat from the north; in 1863 they made a large-scale invasion. While the British government was thinking about giving up all its official connexions, the other European countries who had forts along the coast left. In 1850 the Danes sold their fort of Christiansborg to the British, and in 1872 the Dutch sold Elmina and their other forts and left the coast.

The sale of Elmina led straight to another Ashanti invasion. In 1873 the main Ashanti army advanced into the Protectorate towards the main British fort of Cape Coast, swearing that they would bring its walls back to Kumasi. They failed, partly because torrential rains held up their 1873 attack, and much more especially because the British government at last decided to make a major attack against them in order to obtain a permanent peace. Therefore, in 1874, the Ashanti found themselves faced by an army of British and African troops led by an experienced soldier, Sir Garnet Wolseley. The Ashantis fought bravely, but they never had a chance against the superior weapons of the British. In February 1874 Kumasi was captured and peace was made.

Having conquered the Ashanti and bought the possessions of the Danes and Dutch, the British now decided that they must accept full responsibility for the Gold Coast area. Therefore they definitely annexed the areas whose connexions had previously been by agreement only, and these, together with Lagos, became a crown colony independent of Sierra Leone. No claims to land ownership were made, but the decision was not popular with the Gold Coast people.

AL HAJ UMAR AND THE SUDAN

While British influence increased in the coastal areas a new leader had appeared in the grassland and sand of the Sudan. This was Al Haj Umar, a member of the chief clan of Futa in the west. After going on a pilgrimage to Mecca he returned to Futa Jallon and organised a Muslim training centre. His followers were given not only religious instruction, but also the most modern guns. In the middle of the nineteenth century he started a series of religious conquests. Between 1854 and 1863 he conquered the kingdoms of Kaarta, Segu, and Massina, took Timbuctu, and established the last of the empires of the Sudan. His empire later collapsed partly owing to revolts and partly to the advance of the French in this region.

THE FRENCH IN WEST AFRICA

The French, who were later to become the chief power in the Sudan and the main rivals of the British in West Africa, built up their influence in two directions.

One direction was northwards from the Guinea coast, and between 1838 and 1843 they established a number of trading stations in this region between those of the British.

The second, and more important, direction, was their eastward advance from the area north of Sierra Leone. For centuries the French had held bases in this region, and the chief explorers there between 1818 and 1827 had been the Frenchmen Mollien, De Beaufort and Caillié. But the eastward advance across the Sudan really began in 1854, when the French government sent General Faideherbe to govern Senegal in order to get rid of him from France. Under his governorship French influence extended southwards towards the Gambia River and eastwards into the Sudan. He drove back the attacks of Al Haj Umar, he occupied the port of Dakar, and he tried to provide a good administrative and educational system. After his retirement in 1865 there was no further extension of French claims for nearly fifteen years.

CHAPTER 6

THE PENETRATION OF
EAST AND CENTRAL AFRICA

Most of the outsiders who first penetrated into the interior of East and Central Africa were Arabs in search of gold, slaves and ivory. Let us now look at the east coast where the Omani Arabs reasserted their rule in the early nineteenth century.

ZANZIBAR AND THE COAST

Portuguese power in East Africa north of Mozambique ended when Sultan bin Seif recaptured the coast for the Arabs in his campaign of 1698–9. But the rule of Sultan bin Seif was not very effective, and throughout the eighteenth century the coastal settlements acted as though they were independent and spent most of their time having feuds with one another. This position changed when an exceptionally strong ruler of Oman, called Seyyid Said, decided to make his rule effective in East Africa. In 1832 he selected Zanzibar as his capital because of its central position and fertile soil, and from that time it began to develop as the most important place on the coast. Said's great interest was trade. With Zanzibar as the main base he encouraged Arab traders to go further and further into the interior. Carrying the red flag of Said's authority they penetrated right to the central lakes collecting slaves, ivory, copal and hides for sale through the Zanzibar market. On Zanzibar itself Said made cloves a major export by insisting that three clove trees should be planted for every coconut palm. While more and more goods were produced for sale Seyyid Said made sure that arrangements were made for selling them. Indian merchants, or 'banyans', were encouraged to settle, and connexions were established with European countries too. Between 1833 and 1844 commercial treaties were made with America, Britain and France and later with other countries. Zanzibar began to flourish as it had never flourished before and its influence was felt far inland. But Said never made any definite claims to the interior although he assumed that he was overlord of it. His was a trading empire, and as long as he got his annual taxes from the governors of the coastal towns, and as long as the trade routes to the interior remained active, he was content.

In 1856 Said died, and according to his wishes, the realm of Zanzibar was separated from that of Oman. In Zanzibar he was succeeded by his son Majid. After an uneventful rule, Sultan Majid was followed in 1870 by his younger brother who became Sultan Barghash.

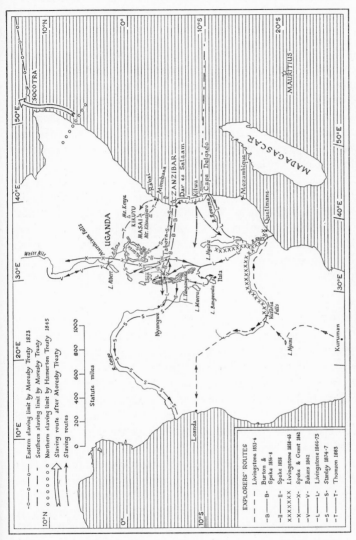

Map 6. East and Central Africa—explorers' journeys and slaving routes
in the nineteenth century.

61

THE EAST AFRICAN SLAVE TRADE

The development of Zanzibar by Said led to the development of the slave trade. This had been going on for centuries but its volume increased as traders penetrated further inland than ever before. Generally Arab slavers avoided the north because of the fierce Masai and Kikuyu. The main caravan routes left from Bagamoyo and Kilwa and made their ways towards Lakes Tanganyika and Nyasa. At bases such as Tabora and Ujiji they exchanged their bales of cloth for slaves, who were forced to carry the ivory tusks back to the coast. From there most slaves were shipped across to the main market of Zanzibar where they were sold to Arabia, India, Mauritius and elsewhere. The suffering was so terrible that most slaves died before they reached Zanzibar, where perhaps 15,000 were sold each year in the early nineteenth century. In the interior slaving had the usual results of encouraging tribal warfare and decreasing the population.

Abolition

The demand to stop the East African slave trade came from the British abolitionists who heard some of the grim details and urged the government to persuade Seyyid Said to abolish it. As a result of their requests Seyyid Said agreed to forbid the export of slaves from Zanzibar to the British territories of India and Mauritius (Moresby Treaty, 1822), and later he went a step further and agreed to forbid their export to his own realm of Oman (Hamerton Treaty, 1845). It was still legal, however, to buy and sell slaves in Zanzibar and along the coast. The Sultan agreed with the restrictions of 1823 and 1845 because the British were the strongest power in the Indian Ocean and their friendship was valuable, but he did not like decreasing the profits from his slave exports, nor did he like becoming unpopular with his subjects who were determined to go on with the trade. In fact they did go on with it regardless of the Moresby and Hamerton treaties. British naval patrols tried to stop them but it was a hopeless task to catch the little dhows in the vastness of the Indian Ocean. So in 1873 the British government gave up its attempts to reduce slaving by restricting the markets. Instead it demanded that the slave trade in East Africa should end entirely, and that the slave markets should be closed. Sultan Barghash at first refused to agree, but owing to the persuasion of the British consul, Sir John Kirk, and the fear that the British navy might compel his agreement if his refusal persisted, Barghash changed his mind. Thus, in June 1873, the export of slaves from any part of the Sultan's dominions became illegal, and all the slave markets were closed. Later on the Christian missions built a church where the Zanzibar slave market had been, and today its altar stands where the whipping post once stood. The 1873 treaty was far more effective than the others had been, although attempts to continue the trade still went on until the railway finally made the whole business unprofitable.

The 1873 treaty did not abolish slavery. That lingered on until 1897 in Zanzibar and longer still upon the mainland, but generally the Arabs did not ill-treat the slaves who worked for them, and many had no wish to leave their masters. It was in the catching and transporting of the slaves that the worst cruelties had existed.

It would be difficult to over-emphasise the importance of the abolition of the slave trade on East Africa's development. It was the condition upon which peace and progress depended.

MISSIONARIES AND EXPLORERS

The growth of the Christian church in East Africa began when the German, Dr Krapf, arrived in Zanzibar for the Church Missionary Society in 1844. Seyyid Said readily gave him permission to try to convert the tribes on the mainland, so Dr Krapf crossed to Mombasa. His efforts and sacrifices were typical of this pioneer period of missionary work. Within a few months the climate killed his wife and child, while he himself lay desperately ill. But he never thought of giving up. Soon he was joined by the Rev. John Rebmann and together they opened a mission station at Rabai near the coast. They did not only preach. They spent years of work on local languages, and they also explored into the interior and reported the snow-capped peaks of Kilimanjaro and Mt Kenya, and stories of lakes in the interior.

Burton, Speke and the Bakers

These reports interested the Royal Geographical Society, and several expeditions went to explore the central lakes. The first, in 1856, was headed by Burton who was led by Arab guides to Lake Tanganyika with which he was delighted. But he became very indignant when his younger companion, Speke, made a personal expedition north to Lake Victoria and said that the Nile probably had its source there. Yet Speke's guess was correct, and he was sent on a journey to prove it. In 1862 he found that the Nile flowed out of the northern end of the lake. He also saw the Kabaka of Buganda and spent a while at his court. As Speke travelled north he met two other English travellers coming south along the Nile. They were Sir Samuel Baker and his wife, who went on to discover Lake Albert and the Murchison Falls.

David Livingstone

While the old, old mystery of the Nile's source was being solved, away to the south the interior was being explored by a man who won the respect of Europe and Africa more than anyone else. His name was Livingstone. This gruff young Scot with an iron will had joined the London Missionary Society's station in Bechuanaland in 1841. He became convinced that the great need was to open the continent for Christianity and peaceful trade, and in any case he loved the thrill and challenge of exploration. Therefore, between 1853 and 1856 he made the first of his three great journeys when he travelled from the middle Zambezi to Loanda on the Atlantic coast and then back across the continent again to Quelimane. On the way he saw the Victoria Falls. From the time of his return he became famous. The interest and sympathy he aroused for Africa and her people were such that a new missionary society (Universities' Mission to Central Africa) was founded to continue his work of opening the continent. Two years later he was off again on his second big journey (1858–63). This time he was employed by the government to see if the Zambezi was a suitable route into the interior. He soon found that because of the rapids it was not suitable for boats, so he turned his interest northwards up the Shiré River, where burnt-out villages and starving people showed the horrible effects of slaving. Here the Universities' Mission followed up and started its first station in 1861, but while Livingstone continued exploring northwards along Lake Nyasa, disease and slaving opposition forced the mission to leave and move to Zanzibar.

When Livingstone returned from this journey he was over fifty but his exploring days were not over yet. Speke and the Bakers had returned to England in 1863 and 1865, reporting that the sources of the Nile lay in Lakes Victoria and Albert, and Livingstone was asked by the Royal Geographical Society to see if there was another source in the region of Lake Tanganyika. Livingstone's last journey began in 1866 from Zanzibar. He travelled inland along the Rovuma River to sort out the complicated network of river sources in Central Africa. But he never did sort them out, although for seven years he explored in all directions until in 1873 his health gave out and he was found dead, kneeling beside his bed in a mud hut at Ilala. Then came the greatest tribute any white man has ever had from Africa—the Africans who had accompanied him carried his body all the way back to Zanzibar for shipment to England. They ran appalling risks, they refused all suggestions made to them to bury the body and have done with it, and eventually they went to England themselves to see their friend's body, which had travelled so far so hard, laid to its final rest at Westminster Abbey.

The geographical discoveries of Livingstone were important, but still more important were the interest and sympathy which he aroused for the African people especially in connexion with the slave trade. His reports had done much to speed up abolition in East Africa in

1873 and his belief that the final answer was to open the continent for 'commerce and Christianity' was widely accepted.

Sir Henry Stanley

The exploration of the watersheds and central lakes of Africa was completed by Stanley. After a youth of hardships and adventures he became famous when he led an expedition on behalf of an American newspaper to Dr Livingstone at Ujiji in 1871. This launched him on a career as an African explorer, and as such he was rough, tough, and very successful. His greatest expedition was from 1874 to 1877 when he confirmed that Lake Victoria, and not Lake Tanganyika, was the Nile source by sailing right round both lakes, after which he showed that the Lualaba River, seen by Livingstone, was part of the Congo by sailing down it to the Atlantic. After his return Leopold of the Belgians hastened to employ him to develop and explore the Congo further (1877–83). In 1887 he made his last expedition through the Congo to the region north of Buganda, where a garrison under Emin Pasha had been cut off by a revolt in the Sudan.

The direct route to Buganda

A very important route, which was still unexplored, was the direct route from Mombasa to Buganda. So far, everyone had reached Buganda from Bagamoyo round the south of Lake Victoria. In 1882 a German, Dr Fischer, attempted the direct route to the north and was turned back by the Masai. A year later an Englishman, Joseph Thomson, attempted it, and on his first attempt the Masai turned him back as well. But he tried again, and on his second attempt he succeeded in crossing what are now the Kenya Highlands to the region of Nyanza. His difficulties were great and he did not give a promising account of what he saw, but nevertheless the highlands he had crossed were later to become a major area of European settlement.

BUGANDA

We have already seen that Buganda, ruled over by the Kabaka assisted by his chiefs, had become the strongest of the Bantu kingdoms in the great lakes area by the time of the arrival of the first Arab traders (about 1848) and the first European explorers (1862). These outside traders and explorers described Buganda as a warlike country which terrorised its neighbours, but they also described the more peaceful arts which had developed there. The Baganda people, they said, had a religion—Lubareism—which was a mixture of witch-craft and ancestor worship; they also had a great love for colourful dress and were experts in beadwork, and their homes were unusual beehive-shaped huts often consisting only of a grass roof supported by poles. The rich and important Baganda people seem to have lived very grandly with large households of wives and slaves, although the peasants and slaves had a very different standard. For them life was hard and cheap. A peasant had to work and fight according to the commands of his chief; a slave might be killed for upsetting his master's wine. Nevertheless, the life of poor people in most coun-tries of the world was hard in the nineteenth century, and the first visitors to Buganda agreed that it was an exceptionally advanced African society.

During Stanley's journey to the central lakes (1874–7) he visited the Kabaka Mutesa. This visit had the effect of speeding up the missionary movement to Buganda because the Kabaka showed great interest in Christianity and Stanley had suggested that missionaries should be sent. It seemed an extraordinary idea because although work had already been started by the Protestant and Catholic missions at the coast, the missionary societies had thought of working their way slowly inland. They had not considered leaping 800 miles into the interior all at once. But missionary pioneers did not lack courage, and by 1876 the first missionaries for the English Church Missionary Society arrived in Buganda. Very soon afterwards French Catholic missionaries of the White Fathers arrived as well. Although Catholic and Protestant missionaries worked without strife in other parts of Africa, in Buganda they were both forced to work side by side at the Kabaka's capital. The results were unfortunate. Sharp differences occurred, and when Mutesa died in 1884 his son Mwanga was not strong enough to hold his people together. As a result they divided into rival parties where politics and religion became hope-lessly mixed up, with the French missionaries on one side and the English on the other. Mwanga attempted to solve his problems by a severe persecution of all Christians which led to the martyrdom of some of the Baganda converts and the murder of Bishop Hannington (1885), but it did not wipe out Christianity; indeed, persecution caused it to spread as people fled from the capital to all parts of the country, and Buganda became one of the most successful areas of missionary work.

Meanwhile the country was in a state of horrible confusion. Mwanga had lost control of his people, and for a while in 1888 the local Arabs actually took his country from him. With the help of the Christian parties he regained it, but soon raids began from Bunyoro. It was at this troubled point in Buganda's history that Britain and Germany entered the scene.

CHAPTER 7

THE PENETRATION OF SOUTH AFRICA

During the early nineteenth century in West and East Africa the main reasons for European interest were the desire to end the slave trade and the desire to encourage peaceful development. But in South Africa, where the climate was better for European settlement, the motives were different. There, the penetration of the interior was largely the result of a desire for land on which to settle. It involved three main forces: (i) the Bantu tribes who were expanding south-wards, (ii) the Boers who were expanding northwards, and (iii) the British who took over the government of the Cape settlement.

THE BRITISH TAKE OVER THE CAPE

The British annexed the Cape settlement in 1795 when the French invaded Holland. From that time, except for a brief period (1802–6) during which it was given back to the Dutch, the Cape became a British possession. It was valued as a calling place for ships on their way to India and the East, and not as an area of settlement. Therefore the European population remained chiefly Dutch. In 1820, however, some settlement by British people did begin when 5000 emigrants from England were landed in the eastern region, at what became Port Elizabeth.

At first the Dutch accepted the British governors and the small administrative changes that were made. They also accepted the arrival of the 1820 settlers from England. But what they would not accept was the attitude of the British towards the Hottentots within the Cape, and towards the Bantu invasions from the north. On these questions the Boers disagreed violently with the British government.

We have seen that although the Boers were not particularly unkind in their treatment of their servants and slaves, they did believe that the Hottentots and coloured folk were inferior to themselves. But we have seen, also, that in Britain there was a great increase of missionary interest, and in South Africa the London Missionary Society began to have a strong influence. The attitude of the British missionaries towards the African people was completely different from that of the Boers. The missionaries' main purpose was to help and protect the Africans—one of them caused a sensation by purchasing and marrying a young slave girl—and this made them hostile to the Boers whom they regarded as oppressors. Strong feelings developed between the Boers and the missionaries especially after the arrival (1819) of Dr John Philip, who superintended the London Missionary Society in South Africa for nearly fifty years. He was a man of strong opinions and he had a strong influence in the government. The three main ways in which the differences of opinion showed were over the questions of the Hottentots, the abolition of slavery, and the frontier.

The Hottentots had ceased to exist as an organised people, and were generally used as servants and slaves by the Boers. This horrified the missionaries. By the 50th Ordinance of 1828, Hottentots were allowed equal rights with Europeans under the law and they could no longer be forced to work for a master unless they wished to do so. The Boers regarded this as 'contrary to the laws of God' and 'intolerable for any decent Christian'. They were very angry.

The second question which increased the Boers' anger was the abolition of slavery in the British Empire which took effect in 1833. The opposition which resulted from this was not so much because the Boers wanted to keep their slaves, but because they thought the compensation which the British paid them was too small. They were also afraid of the increasing number of African and coloured people who were becoming unemployed beggars and likely to commit crimes.

The third question resulted from the disputes over the frontier. We have already seen that the struggle for land between the Bantu and the Boers began in the region of the Great Fish River in 1779. This struggle usually took the form of cattle raids by the Bantu, which were followed by attacks and annexations of land by the settlers. These raids and annexations are usually called the 'Kaffir Wars' and they continued until the last part of the century. One such raid took place in 1834 when 12,000 Bantu warriors raided southwards killing settlers and damaging crops. They were driven back, and the British Governor annexed some of their territory to compensate the settlers who had suffered. This new region of European settlement was to be called Queen Adelaide Province. The British government in England thought this was harsh to the Bantu and therefore the province had to be given up and European settlement there was forbidden.

Many of the frontier Boers thought this was the last straw. They felt that they had been insulted by the 50th Ordinance, cheated by the freeing of the slaves, and now they decided that the British government was not interested in protecting them. Many of them therefore decided to leave the Cape settlement and go inland where the British government could not interfere. So the Great Trek began.

THE GREAT TREK

All the Dutch did not leave with the Great Trek. It was mainly the frontier farmers who were concerned, and they had always disliked government restrictions and they had always been interested in exploring inland for new areas of settlement. The main groups of

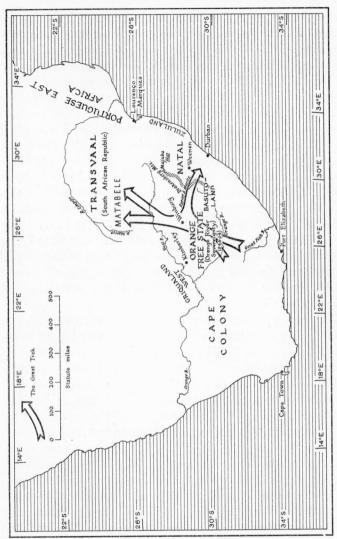

Map 7. The Great Trek in South Africa.

71

trekkers began to move northwards in 1836 and 1837. Their covered waggons pulled by teams of oxen and containing their few possessions bumped their way inland for about 300 miles across the veld. Then they gathered north of the Orange River in a huge camp. Some trekkers stayed in this area which was first known as the Orange River Sovereignty. Others moved even further north and crossed the Vaal. In this region, which developed into the Transvaal, they were fiercely opposed by the Matabele who were defeated and driven north. The main group of trekkers followed their leader, Piet Retief, over the Drakensberg Mountains. These mountains were sometimes so steep that the waggons had to be taken to pieces and lowered bit by bit, but they succeeded in reaching the region of Natal. There, the Zulu king, Dingaan, pretended to welcome them, and persuaded Retief and his men to come to a Zulu feast. But at the feast they were suddenly murdered, and then the Zulus went on to kill the other 300 trekkers who had formed their waggon camp at Weenen. These bloodthirsty happenings caused the Boer trekkers from the Orange and Vaal regions to attack the Zulus, and in 1838 Dingaan was defeated and the Boers occupied Natal.

The Boers were brave, determined people, but their policy of occupying whatever land they wanted and pushing out the Bantu caused unrest on the frontiers of Cape Province because the displaced Bantu tried to come in. To stop this the British government decided to annex Natal as a British colony in 1843, and when the Boers objected to this in 1848 and began to leave, the Cape Governor decided to annex the Orange River Sovereignty as well. In the 1850's, however, the British government decided that the South African possessions were too expensive and must be reduced. Therefore, in 1854, the Orange settlement became independent and was renamed the Orange Free State, although Natal remained British.

Thus, the Great Trek not only led to a fairly quick penetration of the interior; it also divided the once united European settlement of South Africa into two British states (the Cape and Natal) and two Boer states (the Orange Free State and the Transvaal). Most important of all, perhaps, was the fact that the land policy followed by the trekkers and their successors created a dangerous situation by invading Bantu-occupied regions and leaving the Africans with only a very small proportion of the land.

THE SECOND HALF OF THE NINETEENTH CENTURY

After the great upheaval of these events, the thirty years which followed 1854 may be thought of as a settling-down period, although there were plenty of problems and plenty of troubles to deal with. Let us look at this period in connexion with some of the chief men concerned.

Sir George Grey and Federation

Sir George Grey became Governor of the Cape in 1854. In his youth he had helped to explore Australia. In 1854 he was middle-aged, handsome and intelligent. Already he was well known for his governorship of South Australia and New Zealand. As Governor of the Cape he set to work encouraging African development, especially in connexion with agriculture, education and hospitals. His way of dealing with the divisions in South Africa was to try and persuade all the four provinces to join together voluntarily to deal with big questions, while keeping local problems under their own control; in other words he suggested Federation. Perhaps it would have worked, but we shall never know because the British government in England did not approve, and in 1860 Grey ceased to be Governor of the Cape.

Chief Moshesh and the Basutos

Chief Moshesh had developed the Basutos into a nation and ruled them from about 1820 until his death in 1870. He must have been an impressive man for there are now over a thousand descendants who style themselves his sons. Like other Bantu leaders who came in contact with European settlement, Moshesh found that land to which he thought his tribe had rights was being taken by the Boer settlers. Raid followed raid and each time his lands grew smaller.

73

Moshesh, therefore, realising that he could not withstand the Boers and their weapons, appealed to the British for protection in 1868. The British agreed, the Basuto lands were preserved, but the Boers were greatly angered as they had wanted them.

Rhodes and diamonds

In the area of Kimberley in 1867 a child was seen playing with a bright stone. It turned out to be a diamond worth £500. Further discoveries were made, and by 1871 thousands of adventurers had travelled to Kimberley and the area known as Griqualand West, hoping to make their fortunes by discovering diamonds. One of these adventurers was Cecil Rhodes, who was then a youth of less than twenty. He had come to South Africa as a young man, not with the idea of making his fortune, but with the idea of curing his weak chest. He started as a cotton grower in Natal but he quickly joined the crowd going to the Kimberley diamond fields in 1871, and there he was lucky enough to make his fortune—and what a fortune it was! By 1888 he had practically gained a monopoly of South Africa's diamond production and he had also founded a gold-mining company at Johannesburg. He was said to be the richest man in the world with an income of over £100,000 a month. But Rhodes did not use his money on ordinary pleasure, which he considered a waste of time. Even when he went to a dance he said he always chose the ugliest girl to dance with so that he could concentrate more thoroughly on the exercise of dancing. To him, money was a tool with which to achieve his ambition to develop Africa and spread British influence across as much of it as he could. In this task he would go to almost any lengths. Usually his tremendous wealth would buy what he wanted, whether it was land, a treaty, a concession from the government or a railway. But if money failed Rhodes still had great powers of persuasion. It is not surprising that a man with such ambition, such wealth and such determination should have succeeded in becoming Prime Minister of the Cape and the founder of Rhodesia. Nor is it surprising that the Boers found him troublesome. But we are beginning to look too far ahead.

The discovery of diamonds had more important results than that of making Rhodes a rich man. It was the first of South Africa's very lucky economic discoveries. Later gold and uranium were to help, but it was the discovery of diamonds which first made South Africa prosperous. The population increased, interest in the country increased, and Cape Town harbour had to be enlarged to deal with the extra traffic, just at a time when people had expected that its importance would decline because the Suez Canal had been opened (1869). Also, the sudden increase in prosperity made it possible for Cape Colony to pay for its own administration and defence without British aid, and this contributed to the grant of responsible government in 1872. An unfortunate result of the diamond discoveries was the dispute which began over the ownership of the area where they had been found. Obviously it was very valuable and it was claimed by the Transvaal, the Orange Free State, and the Griqua chief, Waterboer. In 1871 it was decided that Waterboer's claim was the best, and he placed the region in the hands of Cape Colony. This decision understandably angered the Boers who regarded it as yet another annexation.

Chief Cetewayo and the Zulu War

The 1870's were uneasy years in South Africa. There was discontent between Boers and British, and at the end of the decade there was fear of a general Bantu rising. The chief cause of discontent between Boers and British was the annexation of the Transvaal in 1877, which was partly due to the desire of the British government to reunite South Africa, and partly to discourage a Bantu attack upon the Transvaal. Here each Boer family lived in isolation upon their farm and administration hardly existed. The particular danger was that Boer expansion into Zululand might cause a war, for the Zulus were a warlike tribe. Since 1873 their chief had been a fierce young man called Cetewayo. He had built up an army of 30,000 men who were not allowed to marry until they had killed a man in war. This made them such dangerous neighbours that in 1879 the Cape Governor ordered them to disband. They refused, and war broke out. The first British army sent against them was massacred and Cetewayo nearly captured Natal, but six months later he was himself defeated and the Zulus were broken up into separate tribes. Four years later Cetewayo was restored, but his restoration was brief and he died in 1884.

Paul Kruger and the First Boer War

When the Zulu danger had gone the Transvaal Boers were more anxious than ever to regain their independence, and they expected to get it when a new government came to power in England in 1880. When they did not get it they attacked the British and defeated them at Majuba Hill, which ended what is known as the First Boer War. As a result the British accepted the Transvaal's independence.

The leader of the rebellion was Paul Kruger. To Rhodes and the British he seemed a very obstinate, annoying old man, but to the Boers he was a character after their own hearts. He had travelled north with the Great Trek when he was only ten years old, and to him it seemed that man was meant to live in the big open spaces of the veld. There he was at home as one of the finest hunters South Africa has produced and there are a multitude of stories of his prowess—how he knew by instinct where big game could be found and where danger lurked; how he chased a lion while being chased himself by an elephant. And even when he became the leader of the Boers he still kept the homely ways of the open-air man. Anyone could always visit him for a talk if he was at home. He regarded the Boers as his family to be protected against dangers and particularly against the danger of British interference. He believed, after Majuba Hill, that the British were weak, and he was quite clear that he would not tolerate interference from them. When such interference came, as it did after the discovery of the gold-fields, the differences between the Boers and British flared up into a major war.

But that is a story for a later chapter.

CHAPTER 8

THE PARTITION OF AFRICA

GENERAL OUTLINE OF EVENTS

So far our story of Africa in the nineteenth century has been mainly about the connexions with Britain. This is because the British had easily the most active interests there until about 1880. Then the picture suddenly changed, and several other European countries decided that African possessions were well worth having. Claims were made, and by the end of the century practically the whole of Africa south of the Sahara was in theory ruled by one or other of the European powers.

This sudden widespread interest had many sources. It had been aroused when explorers and others had shown what the interior was like, and this led on to a desire for colonies in the hope that they would bring wealth and political power. The countries mainly concerned were Germany, France, Britain and Belgium. The Portuguese were involved as well, but they were too weak to do anything except try to hold what they had.

We might say that the 'scramble for Africa' began in 1876, when Leopold of the Belgians started the International Association for the Exploration and Civilisation of Africa. This sounded very grand, and it did in fact send several expeditions into the interior, one of them on elephants which caused great excitement. But events really began to speed up when the Germans made claims to territories in West, South West, and East Africa between 1883 and 1885. This took the British and French by surprise and they hastened to make official claims as well to areas with which they were concerned.

These rival claims might easily have led to war but in fact they did not. One of the factors which helped to prevent strife was the Berlin Conference (1884–5) which was attended by the European countries concerned with partition, and settled several difficult points in connexion with West Africa and the Congo. At the conference Leopold

77

of the Belgians was recognised as ruler of the area south of the Congo which became the Congo Independent State, and the French were recognised as the rulers of the region north of the river which became the French Congo. Besides settling disputes the Berlin Conference also agreed to various principles. One was that no country could claim a region as a 'sphere of influence' unless it could show evidence of its influence there, and this led to a great interest in making treaties with African chiefs which were often meaningless. Another principle agreed upon was that free trade should be allowed in each region, but this was not often observed in fact.

While politicians, traders, and adventurers were busily partitioning the continent and African chiefs were wondering what all the fuss was about, a conference of a rather different kind was being held at Brussels. The Brussels Conference (1889–90) had three aims and they were all kindly ones—to destroy the African slave trade finally, to protect the African population, and to ensure for Africa the benefits of peace and civilisation. This was encouraging evidence that when Europeans thought of Africa there was goodwill as well as the desire for gain.

The results of Africa's partition were partly good and partly bad. They were good in so far as they speeded the development of the interior and opened it for the benefits of trade and civilisation. They were bad in so far as they made the African people hostile because they did not like the European annexations of land and they did not like the restrictions which were imposed upon them. The process of partition was not particularly popular from the African point of view despite the benefits which accompanied it.

Let us now see how the process of partition worked in some of the different parts of Africa.

WEST AFRICA

The political divisions of West Africa are like fingers stretching inland from the sea. They are not natural divisions for they take no notice of geography and no notice of tribes. They are simply the politicians' answer to the rival claims put forward by Germany, Britain and France as they tried to expand inland from their coastal bases. Let us see how those claims were made.

The French and British had connexions with West Africa before 1880. So had the Germans to a lesser extent, because they had restarted their trade with the coast in the middle of the century. But it came as a surprise when a German expedition landed at various points on the coast in 1884, made treaties with local African chiefs, and then successfully claimed the regions of Togoland and the Cameroons as German Protectorates. Thinking that Germany might also claim the Niger Delta, the British hastily made an official claim to the whole region from the Cameroons to Lagos for themselves, and this became the Oil Rivers Protectorate (renamed the Niger Coast Protectorate in 1893). The French too became alarmed. Their forts, which had been left to the care of a few merchants, were promptly taken over by the French government, and claims to the areas which lay behind them were made. So between 1887 and 1893 the French colonies of French Guinea and the Ivory Coast began. Dahomey also became French despite the vigorous opposition of the African king.

However, the main direction of French expansion was not northwards from the coast but eastwards from Senegal across the Sudan by way of the Niger. In 1883 Bamako was occupied, in 1893–4 Timbuctu itself surrendered to a force of only nineteen men, and by 1896 Say was reached. In this advance the last remnants of Umar's empire disappeared, and the main resistance came from a fierce Mandingo king, Samory, who opposed the French for sixteen years until his final exile in 1898.

The French advance had the effect of limiting British and German expansion into the interior and made necessary a series of treaties to fix the frontiers. Those of Gambia and Sierra Leone were settled in 1889 and 1895 respectively, but we must look more closely at the events in the Gold Coast and Niger areas.

In the region of the Gold Coast the 1874 war had left the Ashanti people restless and disunited, but at last they found in King Prempeh

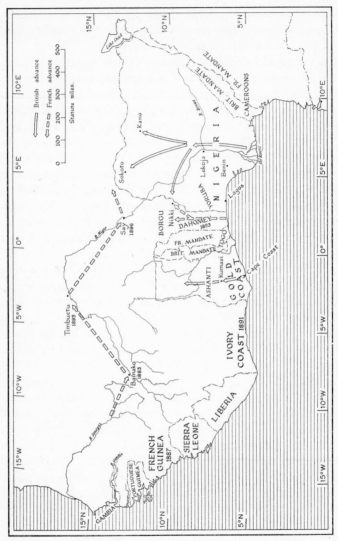

Map 8. The partition of West Africa by the European powers.

an Asantehene whom they liked and they enthroned him upon the Golden Stool of Kumasi. Unfortunately he was so warlike and practised human sacrifice on such a large scale that the British in the south became alarmed. As the British were already alarmed by the French advance in the north and the possibility of German expansion from Togoland they made an expedition to Kumasi in 1896 which dethroned Prempeh and established a Protectorate over the Ashantis and the region to the north. This arrangement only lasted four years and then a foolish demand by the British Governor for the Golden Stool provoked another Ashanti war. This resulted in the defeat of the Ashantis and in 1901 the country was annexed as a crown colony.

Further eastwards, in what is now Nigeria, the Colony of Lagos expanded to include the Yorubaland Protectorate (1896) and Benin was taken (1897) to end the slaving and human sacrifice which still persisted there. But the main struggle was for the Niger itself and the lands to its north. These became British largely due to the efforts of a rich, strange, hawk-like man called Sir George Taubman Goldie, who once spent three years in the desert with the Bedouin for love of an Arab girl. He visited the delta in 1877 and saw the trading rivalry which existed there between the French and British Companies. To end this he bought up the French trading concerns and gained a monopoly of the Niger trade. From 1882 this was controlled by his National Africa Company. His activities were not confined to trade, however, for he was also interested in abolishing slaving and after much persuasion in 1886 he got permission to exercise administrative powers on behalf of the British government in the regions where he traded in the north. At the same time his Company became the Royal Niger Company. Most of the Company's trade was in the delta region but it had an inland post at Lokoja and its agents had gone even further north and made agreements with the Fulani emirs of Sokoto and other states. This caused disputes with the French which were settled in 1890 when the French agreed not to claim regions south of an imaginary line stretching from Say to Lake Chad, which left them only with the desert to the north. But this agreement only settled the northern frontier. The western boundaries were still disputable, and to prevent French expansion here a special army was started known as the West African Frontier Force.

By the end of the century the responsibilities of the Company had increased so much that the British government itself decided to take over the administration of the Protectorate of Northern Nigeria from the Company. This took effect from 1900, and the first High Commissioner for the Northern Protectorate was Sir Frederick Lugard who had previously commanded the West African Frontier Force. As Lagos and the Niger Coast Protectorate (now renamed the Protectorate of Southern Nigeria) were already ruled by the British government this brought the whole of what is now Nigeria under their control.

EAST AND CENTRAL AFRICA

In West Africa the effect of partition was to increase European claims and influence and to fix more definitely the areas which each country administered. In East Africa the position was different. There, no European country had any claims or possessions north of Mozambique before 1885 and the accepted ruler was the Sultan of Zanzibar whose independence Britain and France had recognised in a declaration made in 1862.

But Sultan Barghash was most unfortunate, for it was his unlucky chance to be ruler when the power of Zanzibar collapsed. When he became Sultan of Zanzibar in 1870 his influence was felt so far inland that people said 'When one pipes in Zanzibar, they dance at the lakes. When he died in 1888 that influence had gone, not through any fault of Barghash, but because of increased European interest in his dominions which led to annexations there.

Sultan Barghash and Britain

We have already seen that Zanzibar had been made a busy commercial centre by Seyyid Said. Its connexions with Europe increased still further when the Suez Canal was opened in 1869, and during

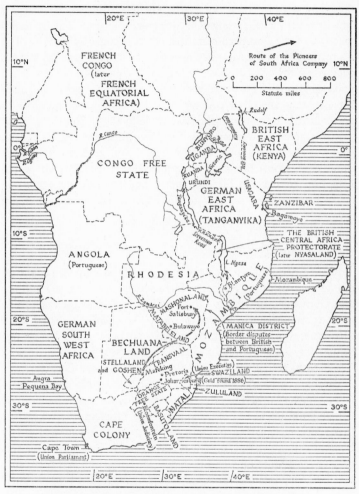

Map 9. The partition of East, Central and South Africa.

the 1870's expeditions and traders from Belgium, France and Germany were active in the Sultan's lands. Barghash watched this activity with mixed feelings: he welcomed the trade but he feared that one of the European countries might become too interested in his territories and start annexing them, in which case he had no adequate army or navy to drive them off. For protection he relied upon the British. They had sent more explorers, traders and missionaries than any other country, and they had been responsible for persuading him to abolish the slave trade in 1873. But the greatest British connexion was through Sir John Kirk, the British consul, who was Barghash's most trusted friend and adviser. In view of these connexions Barghash had hoped that the British would help him to develop his dominions, but they refused to take any direct responsibility for fear of the expense and trouble it might involve.

Germany claims Usagara

In 1885 Barghash's fears came true; one of the European countries did annex part of his territory. The country was Germany and the area Germany claimed was Usagara which lay across the main trade route from Bagamoyo to the interior. The claim was based upon silly treaties with local chiefs which had been made by an unscrupulous young German named Carl Peters, but Germany forced Barghash to accept them by threatening to bombard Zanzibar.

Barghash and Kirk had expected British help against outside interference such as this. They did not get it. This was partly because the British government had other more serious problems to deal with at that time, such as the Mahdist revolt in the Sudan, and partly because Britain wished to remain friendly with Germany. This was very disappointing for the Sultan and for Kirk, who was quite sure that Germany intended to annex all the Sultan's mainland territory.

The 1886 Partition Treaty

As a result of Kirk's views, in 1886 the British government made

a treaty with Germany which divided the Sultan's mainland possessions into a British sphere which became British East Africa (later
renamed Kenya), and a German sphere which became German East
Africa (later renamed Tanganyika). As in Nigeria and Rhodesia the
British left further development to a private company known as the
Imperial British East African Company or IBEA. The Germans also
left their sphere to a company at first until an Arab rebellion—which
made all Europeans in East and Central Africa very unpopular—
caused the German government to take it over.

The 1890 Heligoland Treaty

Although the 1886 treaty prevented Germany from annexing the
whole mainland it was not a final settlement, for nothing had been
said about boundaries in the west. In particular nothing had been
said about Uganda, so Carl Peters made an expedition there and tried
to claim it for Germany. But this time Peters' claim failed because
in 1890 the British and German governments made what is called the
Heligoland Treaty. By this treaty Uganda became a British sphere
and Zanzibar became a British Protectorate. In return for these
concessions Germany was given a little island called Heligoland in
the waters off northern Europe.

What were the results of this partitioning of East Africa? Certainly it speeded up the pace of development, but equally certainly
it aroused suspicion in the minds of the African people about their
land. So far as Zanzibar was concerned its importance was over, for
its main wealth had come from the products of the mainland and
these it no longer controlled.

Uganda becomes a Protectorate (1894)

In Uganda the Heligoland Treaty led to further excitement. The
Imperial British East Africa Company, which was already responsible for British East Africa, became responsible for Uganda too in
1890. The Company's capital was small and its profits were smaller,
but it sent a young officer, Captain Lugard (whom we have met

already in connexion with his later work in West Africa) with a very inadequate force to establish its authority in the Kabaka's kingdom. Lugard succeeded in getting the Kabaka, Mwanga, to recognise the Company's authority and he succeeded in defeating the Muslim raiders from Bunyoro. However, he could not prevent a serious civil war between the Fransa party (favoured by the French Catholic missionaries) and the Ingleza party (favoured by the English Protestant missionaries). By the end of 1892, with the aid of Sudanese troops from the north, Lugard had established order again, but by this time the Company was bankrupt and so he was ordered to withdraw. This withdrawal was indignantly opposed in Britain because the C.M.S. said that their missionaries would be driven out if Lugard's troops withdrew, and politicians said that some other European power would take over Uganda and get control of the headwaters of the Nile. As a result of this opposition Uganda officially became a British Protectorate in 1894 and the Company gave up its responsibilities there.

British East Africa becomes a Protectorate (1895)

A year later the British government also took over British East Africa as a Protectorate as the Company came to an end. Unlike the Companies in Nigeria and Rhodesia, the East Africa Company had never been very profitable. It had been run mainly by wealthy men who were sincerely anxious to help African development; Sir William Mackinnon who was its chairman, and Sir John Kirk who was a director, were typical members.

Nyasaland and Central Africa

Further south the region around Lake Nyasa was in dispute. British interest there had been aroused by Livingstone's Zambezi expedition (1858–63) and by the Universities' Mission. Although this mission had been forced to withdraw to Zanzibar, work was resumed in the Nyasa region when the Scottish Church succeeded in starting a permanent mission at Blantyre in the Shiré Highlands in

1876. They were followed by a missionary trading company which put boats on Lakes Nyasa and Tanganyika and built the Stevenson road joining the lakes in an attempt to oppose the large-scale slaving which still went on in the region. In 1883 a consul was appointed.

The Portuguese did not like this British activity at all. They wanted to join Mozambique to Angola and thus form a solid Portuguese block across Central Africa, so they resented the British intruders and claimed the Shiré region as part of Mozambique. In 1889 matters came to a head when the British consul, Sir Harry Johnston, declared a Protectorate over Blantyre, whereupon a Portuguese expedition, led by the swashbuckling Portuguese explorer Serpa Pinto, prepared to capture Blantyre by force. To make matters worse, soon after this Rhodes' South Africa Company began advancing into Rhodesia and threatened the western borders of Mozambique. Portugal may have been small and weak but her people's blood was up. To avoid war, negotiations began between Britain and the Portuguese governments and by the 1891 Anglo-Portuguese Treaty the whole area north of the Zambezi was divided into the frontiers which still remain. The British Central Africa Protectorate (later renamed Nyasaland) was administered by the British government, and the region to the west by the South Africa Company. The frontiers of northern Rhodesia were modified by a further treaty in 1892 when King Leopold of the Belgians astutely acquired for his Congo Free State the extremely valuable mining region of Katanga which had just been discovered.

But the mention of Rhodesia has already led us towards the partition of South Africa to which we must now turn.

SOUTH AFRICA

German South West Africa

Until the 1880's the three main groups of people influencing South Africa were the Bantu, the Boers and the British, but in 1883 the Germans also became interested. This alarmed the British who regarded them as rivals, and pleased the Boers who regarded them as

allies. A few German missionaries and traders had settled in Damara-
land and Namaqualand in south-west Africa in the middle of the
nineteenth century. The British government at the Cape had refused
to give them protection because they were north of the Orange River,
but it came as a surprise when a German expedition landed at
Angra Pequena Bay in 1883 and successfully claimed a Protectorate
over what became German South West Africa.

The British were particularly alarmed by this move because the
Transvaal Boers were also expanding. Their expansion was directed
east and west. In the east a group of Boers had broken from the
Transvaal and claimed a large part of Zululand, where they started
what they called 'The New Republic' of 1884. Perhaps they had
hoped to reach the sea, but between 1886 and 1887 the British made
this impossible by reducing the size of the New Republic, which
became part of the Transvaal, and by annexing Zululand.

The western expansion of the Boers was regarded particularly
seriously because their two new settlements of Stellaland and
Goshen lay across the route from Cape Province to the north.
When the Germans claimed South West Africa the British feared
the route might be completely closed and they quickly annexed
Bechuanaland.

The British South Africa Company and Rhodesia

One of the men responsible for the annexation of Bechuanaland
was Rhodes. Rhodes had a special interest in the region because his
great plan was to develop the northern area by means of the British
South Africa Company for which he obtained a charter in 1889. The
most powerful Bantu people already in the northern region were the
Matabele, so treaties were made with their great king, Lobengula,
which granted the Company special rights to land and minerals.
Then, in 1890, the pioneers of Rhodes' Company began to move
northwards from Mafeking and established Fort Salisbury. With
Rhodes' wealth supporting it development was swift; communications by rail and telegraph were provided and settlers began to farm
the land.

While Rhodes was delighted, others were not. The Portuguese had hoped that they would be able to form a solid block across Central Africa by joining Angola to Mozambique. When Rhodesia began, these hopes were destroyed, but the Portuguese did not submit without opposition and some sharp little fights occurred in the Manica region before a boundary agreement was made with them in 1891. The Matabele also disliked the increasing settlement, and in 1893 Lobengula could restrain them no longer and war began. When it ended Lobengula was dead, Matabeleland came under Company control, and plans were made to build a town at the royal village of Bulawayo. But that was not the end of Matabele opposition. In 1896 they rose again, supported by the Mashonas, until Rhodes went northwards to negotiate with them himself unarmed in the Matoppo Hills. He brought peace, he provided food, and he won their respect to such an extent that, when he died five years later, the Matabele gave him their royal salute, which they had never given to any white man before.

The discovery of gold, and the Jameson Raid

While the partition of South Africa was taking place a tremendous discovery was made in the Transvaal. In 1885–6 gold was found on the Witwatersrand, and the gold-rush city of Johannesburg began. President Kruger and the Boers were interested in independence and in farming; they distrusted industrialisation and they were quite content to let the gold discoveries be developed by the foreigners, or 'Uitlanders', who came pouring in, especially as they increased the Transvaal's revenue from under £200,000 in 1885 to over £4,000,000 in 1889. But President Kruger would not grant the Uitlanders any rights because he said they were not permanent residents and might go at any moment leaving just their holes in the ground. This situation, together with other incidents, led to the Jameson Raid (December 1895 to January 1896) when a force led by the administrator of Rhodesia, Dr Jameson, attempted to invade and capture Johannesburg on the Uitlanders' behalf. This was a horrible failure. Rhodes, who was the Prime Minister of the Cape, resigned because he had encouraged Jameson's plan. The Boers naturally became very suspicious and hostile, and Kruger prepared for war. Attempts at reconciliation during the next few years failed, and at the end of 1899 the Boer War began.

The Boer War (1899–1902)

The Jameson Raid was far from being the only cause of the war. The independent Boer farmers had always disliked British interference, and those in the Transvaal had resented the way in which the British had annexed the regions around them, leaving no outlet to the sea. When the Jameson Raid won him more support than he had ever had before Kruger realised that his time was ripe.

The actual fighting lasted three years. It was between the British and the Boers; the Bantu remained neutral, at least in theory. Although the Boers of the Orange Free State and the Transvaal fought bravely and were at first successful, they stood no chance against the major effort which was made against them in February 1900 when Lord Roberts' army crossed the Orange and marched inexorably north. Within nine months the main Boer army under General Botha had been defeated, and the Transvaal had been overrun, although groups or 'commandos' of Boers continued to make raids until peace was finally signed at Vereeniging in 1902. By this peace the Orange Free State and the Transvaal became British colonies, but they were promised responsible government later; also the British gave £3,000,000 to help restoration. This very generous peace was one of the good results of the war. Another good result was the starting of the international Boy Scouts Association (1908) by Major Baden Powell, whose defence of Mafeking had made him a tremendous hero.

Reconstruction and Union

The generous peace made reconstruction and reconciliation possible. The man who actually managed the policy after the war was Lord Milner, whose wisdom helped to set South Africa upon its feet again, economically and socially. The mines began to produce once more, administration was improved, and the Boer leaders began to realise the genuine goodwill which existed. The process was carried further when the Transvaal and Orange Free State were granted responsible government (1906–7), and the final step came when union was achieved in 1910. Let us look at this more closely.

The idea of union was not a new one. Sir George Grey had suggested Federation in the 1850's and others later had seen that some kind of union would have advantages in dealing with South Africa's problems. Lord Milner had certainly worked towards it in his post-war administration, and his work bore fruit when representatives from the four provinces met to discuss the question in 1908. Agreement was reached, and plans for union were passed in the South Africa Act which became effective in 1910.

By the South Africa Act supreme authority over all the four provinces of the Union was given to the Union Parliament which was to consist of a Senate and House of Assembly. The head of the Executive side of the government was the Governor-General representing the Crown and he was assisted by an Executive Council chosen from the Parliamentary leaders. A special feature of the act was the division of the capital into three with the Parliament at Cape Town, the Executive at Pretoria, and the Judiciary (head law courts) at Bloemfontein. Special clauses of the act were the recognition of both English and Dutch as official languages, and the recognition of the right to vote for some African coloured people in Cape Province. These clauses could only be altered by a two-thirds majority of Parliament.

The general effect of the South Africa Act was to give the control of South Africa's affairs entirely to the Boers (we shall call them Afrikaners after this) and British who lived there. In chapter 13 we shall see how they got on with each other and how they used their power in relation to the Bantu, who had practically no part in the government themselves and who formed the vast majority of the population.

PART IV

THE PROGRESS OF AFRICA

INTRODUCTION

After the partition of Africa almost the whole continent south of the Sahara was in theory governed by European countries. At first this did not mean very much to the African people because the number of European administrators, traders and missionaries was usually very small indeed and huge areas never even saw a white man. But during the first half of this century the effects of European government have been increasing at a tremendous speed so that today people in most parts of Africa have had their way of life seriously changed. Large modern cities stand where men hunted and lions roamed in the bush, and railways run where slave caravans used to march. In a single lifetime much of Africa has travelled through a thousand years of progress.

In this great journey three main stages may be seen: the first stage was the establishment of law and order; the second was—and is— the process of economic and social development; the third is the attainment of independence. Let us look briefly at each.

The first task which the European powers attempted after partition was that of making their rule effective over the areas they had claimed. This was often opposed by African chiefs who did not understand the treaties—if any—which they had signed, and were naturally indignant at having their authority taken by European intruders. Sometimes fighting took place as in Northern Nigeria and Rhodesia; sometimes chiefs gave way peacefully to the greater force of the European invaders; in either case the process of making European rule effective went on steadily, covering more and more of the interior. It was not a popular process but it brought the advantage of a greater degree of peace and order than the African kings had been strong enough to impose.

The second task was to encourage development. At the Brussels Conference the European powers had promised to bring the benefits of European civilisation to Africa, as well as getting profits from African trade. This meant developing economic resources by encouraging mining and agriculture and by providing roads and railways to carry people and goods. It meant providing hospitals and schools, and in these two activities the missions made—and still make—a vital contribution, for the great majority of schools and hospitals were started by them. At first they were the pioneers; now they are more the specialist helpers.

The cost of providing these things for the millions of Africans who needed them was much higher than the European countries at first realised, but in time it became clear that much more money would have to be lent or given if social and economic development was to go forward at any speed. Britain made a start in 1929 by the Colonial Development Act which made a grant from Britain to help colonial development. The amount of financial help given increased greatly after the 1939–45 war and France, Belgium, and Portugal as well as Britain have all launched increasingly generous development schemes in their territories. The United Nations have also given some financial help, especially through the International Bank for Reconstruction and Development which began just after the war, and has attracted considerable money from the United States of America.

As a result of the economic and social development which has taken place, an educated and wealthy class of Africans developed. They have become doctors, lawyers and teachers. They have also taken an increasing part in the government of their territories, and in some cases they have taken it over completely.

The pace of development has depended to a great extent on the wealth of the colony and the wealth of the European country concerned. It is not strange that the Gold Coast, with its large income from cocoa and minerals, should have become the first European colony to gain complete self-government and become the state of

Ghana. Neither is it strange, in view of Portugal's small resources, that the Portuguese territories are so far behind that an educated class of Africans hardly exists there and the demand for self-government has been retarded.

In some areas the situation has been made difficult by European and Asian settlement. In every case the settlers are far outnumbered by the Africans, but in different parts of Africa different approaches to this have been made. In South Africa the European community intend to keep complete control of the Union and enforce a policy of separating the races from one another. In the Central African Federation a more moderate position has been taken. In Kenya there is a government largely under African control.

Another interesting point in development has been the recent policy of African states to get together. The year 1958 showed this very clearly with the first Conference of Independent African States at Accra, the founding of the Pan-African movement of East and Central Africa in Tanganyika, and the All African Peoples' Conference which was again held at Accra. The states of Africa south of the Sahara are very interested in one another, for they have many common problems.

Having glanced at some of the general points, let us now have a closer look at the progress of each part of the continent.

CHAPTER 9

WEST AFRICA

The states of West Africa have not made their way towards independence at a walking pace—they have run. This does not mean that the European powers who claimed them during the partition period all followed the same policy, for in fact France, Britain, and Germany each tackled the problem of administration in a different way.

THE GERMANS IN TOGOLAND AND THE CAMEROONS

The Germans were the least successful. They tried to govern Togoland and the Cameroons as though they had conquered the African
people living there. Tribal organisation was set aside, the authority
of the chiefs was set aside, and German officials attempted to enforce
a completely new method of rule. This naturally aroused opposition.
As the same policy, with the same result, was followed in German
East Africa and South West Africa the German Parliament attempted
to make reforms from 1907. Some reforms were made, but in 1914
war started in Europe and as a result the French and British in
Africa attacked the German territories and quickly captured them.
When peace was made in Europe after Germany's defeat in 1918,
the conquered German colonies were placed in the care of an international organisation known as the League of Nations, which
requested Britain and France to undertake the administration of
these colonies as 'mandates'. The final authority over the mandates,
however, remained with the League of Nations to whom reports
had to be sent each year stating what progress had taken place in
African development. By this arrangement the eastern part of Togoland and the eastern part of the Cameroons were entrusted to French
control and were administered by the French as separate colonies.
The western parts were entrusted to the British, and were, in effect,
added on to the Gold Coast and Nigeria.

BRITISH POLICY

The British, at first, had no special theory about governing their
African territories. When the various areas became British colonies,
officials were sent out; District Officers were sent to do the local
administrative work and a Governor supervised them. But it
happened that Sir Frederick Lugard, who had been appointed High
Commissioner of the Northern Protectorate of Nigeria in 1900, found
that he had too few assistants and too little money with which to
administer his region. He also found that the Fulani emirs of the
north were strong rulers, and after making them accept his authority

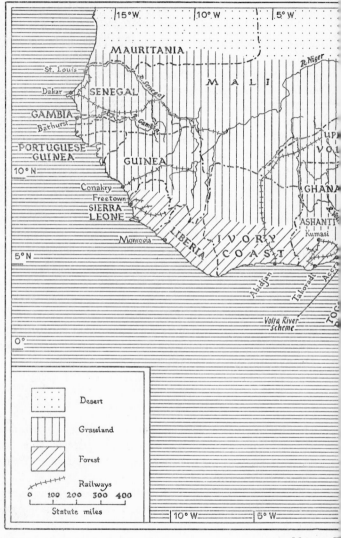

Map 10. W

96

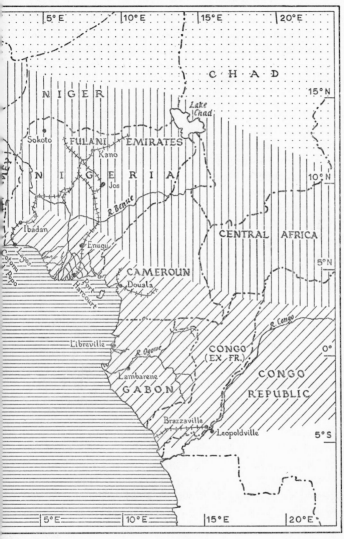

rica today.

97

in 1903 Lugard took an unexpected step. Instead of dismissing them he left them as rulers on condition that they ended such practices as slaving, and accepted the supervision of a British official called a Resident, who only interfered to check abuses or give advice. This arrangement of supervising existing rulers was called 'Indirect Rule'. The British government thought that as it worked so well in Northern Nigeria it would also work throughout their other African colonies. They found, however, that its success really depended on the strength of the authority of the African rulers. Where African rulers were strong (as they were in Northern Nigeria) and where tribal loyalty was clear (as it was with the Ashanti of the Gold Coast) indirect rule was successful. But where tribes had been broken up (as in the southern part of Nigeria) and where there were numerous educated Africans (as in the coastal region of the Gold Coast) the Africans did not particularly want to revive the power of the chiefs, even if chiefs whom they would respect could have been found. Despite these differences indirect rule became the general policy of the British towards their African colonies.

So far as the central government is concerned this is a convenient place to explain very briefly the general system of constitutional development in British territories in Africa. The British aimed at making each region able to look after its own affairs by developing the central government in each territory. At the head of each territory was placed a Governor who was responsible to the Colonial Secretary in the British government. At first the Governor was the main power in each region, and his advisers became the official Executive Council. But the most interesting feature of government was the development of a Legislative Council. In most cases this started by having members chosen by the Governor simply to give advice or because of their official position (officials). However, they were expected to develop into Councils which were elected and which would control legislation with the chief members as Ministers in charge of departments. This process has been completed already in some territories—with West Africa leading the way; in other territories it is still developing.

Legislative Councils began in Gambia in 1843, the Gold Coast in 1850, Lagos in 1862, and Sierra Leone in 1863, but until Africans were used to British ways, and until enough of them were educated to take part in debates, the African people were not directly represented. By 1925, however, African elected representatives were sitting in the West African Legislatures, and by 1948 the elected members were a majority in the Legislative Councils of each British West African territory. Final control of affairs still remained with the British government, however, until in 1957 the Gold Coast became completely independent and renamed itself Ghana. At first its position was that of a Dominion, but in 1960 it became a Republic within the British Commonwealth.

Ghana

The African who led the Gold Coast to independence was Dr Kwame Nkrumah. As a political leader he succeeded in arousing tremendous enthusiasm. Partly this was due to his ability, hard work and organisation; he paid visits to the Gold Coast villages and towns complete with loud speakers, caravans, uniforms and slogans. Partly it was also due to his simple friendly interest in all the people. It is said that when people recognised his car they would polish it with their robes as a sign of respect, and that Nkrumah himself would not hesitate to share a meal with a beggar or chat by the roadside with anyone who wanted to talk to him.

Dr Nkrumah was educated locally at mission schools and at Achimota College. Then a wealthy uncle helped him to go to the U.S.A. where he obtained four degrees before going on to further studies in England. In 1947—by which time he had been away twelve years—the Gold Coast African Nationalist leader invited him to return as secretary of the party. Dr Nkrumah accepted. Within a few months of his return serious riots broke out, and for a short time he was among the political leaders who were exiled to the north. The British government tried to put matters right by setting up a committee of enquiry whose members were all Africans, and this committee recommended a new constitution giving a far greater share in the government to the African people. Dr Nkrumah, who had returned from exile and started a new party known as the Convention Peoples' Party (or C.P.P.) won the 1951 elections by a large majority. He was in prison at the time because he had encouraged a general strike, but the Governor wisely released him. In 1952 he officially became Prime Minister. His party had aimed at getting independence rapidly, but there was fear that if the advance was too rapid the north might be upset. However, the 1956 elections showed that Dr Nkrumah's party had a large majority and independence followed in 1957.

Nigeria

Nigeria gained its independence a little later than the Gold Coast. One of the most obvious things about Nigeria is its tremendous size, and we have seen that in 1900 it was divided into three for administrative purposes—the Southern Protectorate, the Northern Protectorate, and the Colony of Lagos. In 1906 Lagos became part of the Southern Protectorate, and in 1914 the two Protectorates united under a Governor-General, Lord Lugard. This had definite economic advantages but there were still big differences between the Sudan region of the north ruled mainly through Muslim emirs, the southwestern region where the Yoruba are the main tribe, and the eastern region where the tribes are more mixed.

An important step in the development of the government was made in 1946 when the Legislative Assembly was made more representative and Houses of Assembly were started in the northern, western and eastern regions. This constitutional arrangement was expected to last for ten years, but as a result of African demands it was altered in 1950 and again in 1954. The alterations of 1954 established a Federation of Nigeria, by which general matters—such as dealings with foreign countries—were left to the Federal Legislature at Lagos to which each region sent representatives. Except for these general matters each region was to look after its own affairs. As each region was developing at a different speed, each obtained independence for its own affairs in turn. Completely responsible government for the whole Federation took place in 1960, with Sir Abubakar Tafawa Balewa as Prime Minister.

Sierra Leone

In Sierra Leone, as in the Gold Coast and Nigeria, there are big social and geographical differences. The Colony around the capital of Freetown has a population who are descendants of freed slaves; they are known as Creoles or Sierra Leoneans. The Protectorate of Sierra Leone, which lies inland from the Colony and is much larger, has an African population which has descended from the original inhabitants. At first the British government showed more interest in the Colony because more progress had been made there, but in the early 1950's the number of members representing the Protectorate in the Legislative Council was considerably increased. By the constitution of 1958 the House of Representatives, which replaced the Legislative Council, had most of its elected members from the Protectorate. At the same time the Executive Council were all unofficial members from the Sierra Leone People's Party led by Sir Milton Margai, a gentle, middle-aged doctor of medicine who for twenty-two years had served as a medical officer in the Sierra Leone Civil Service. He became the Prime Minister, and in 1960, at the age of sixty-four, he travelled to England to request independence for his country. This was attained in 1961.

Gambia

This narrow strip along the Gambia River is the smallest of the British-influenced territories in West Africa. The Colony at the mouth and the Protectorate came under one government in 1935, and today they are ruled by a Governor assisted by a Legislative Council and an Executive Council. The power of Africans in both these councils was increased by a new constitution which took effect from 1954. Gambia has not yet become self-governing—independence might not be easily maintained in so small a region—but African nationalist parties are active there as elsewhere.

THE FRENCH AND WEST AFRICA

After a number of frontier adjustments, by the middle of this century French West Africa consisted of eight territories: Senegal, French Sudan, Mauritania, French Guinea, the Ivory Coast, Upper Volta, Dahomey, and Niger. Togoland and Cameroon were in French trusteeship for the United Nations.

Whereas the British generally encouraged traditional African rulers and hoped that British administration would some day be taken over by the Africans themselves, the French at first followed a quite different policy. They believed that it was best to encourage the African people to accept French ways of life, and for the African territories to become, as it were, an extra part of France. So, in the first part of this century, the government of French West Africa was mainly run from France itself through French officials in the territories. At the head was the Minister for the Colonies who was responsible for all French overseas possessions in Africa and elsewhere. He was a member of the French government—to which the French West African territories sent representatives—and he lived in Paris. Under him came the Governor-General of French West Africa who was responsible for the French West African possessions; he lived in Dakar. Under the Governor-General came the Governors of the eight territories, and each territory was itself divided for administration into districts and subdistricts known as 'Cercles' and 'Subdivisions'.

At first the Africans took little part in the government, but after the Second World War (1939–45) more control was given to the various territories over their own affairs, and more representation was given to the African people. In 1946 a Grand Council was started representing all the French West African territories, and at the same time Territorial Assemblies were set up in each territory.

The French Community and the Republics

The main constitutional advance came in 1958, when, after a series of short, weak governments, the people of France called upon General de Gaulle to be their President and a new constitution was set up. By this constitution the French overseas territories were given the chance of becoming a part of the 'French Community'. This Community was headed by the President, General de Gaulle, together with an Executive Council and a Senate in both of which were representatives of each state which joined the Community. French Guinea rejected the whole constitution and became completely independent under its African Prime Minister, Sekou Touré. The other French West African territories, however, decided to remain within the Community, mostly as Republics. In 1959 Senegal and Sudan combined to form the Federation of Mali, which became independent within the French Community in June 1960, but a few months later Senegal and Sudan separated from each other again. In August 1960 Ivory Coast, Upper Volta, Dahomey and Niger also became independent within the French Community and together formed the 'Entente'. The Community therefore looks like developing into something like the British Commonwealth which also includes a number of independent states with close associations.

GABON, THE REPUBLIC OF THE CONGO, THE CENTRAL AFRICAN REPUBLIC AND CHAD

It is convenient at this point to deal with the states which used to form French Equatorial Africa. French traders and missionaries had been active in the Gabon area for many years before its king officially transferred his kingdom to France in 1839. Libreville, the capital, was started in 1848 when a number of freed slaves were landed there, and some years later Europe and America became interested when the French explorer Du Chaillu brought back the first specimens of gorillas from this region. During the 1860's and 1870's explorers made their ways along the Ogowé to the Congo, and during the period of partition the French explored and claimed the regions further north towards Lake Chad. At first the administration of the French Congo was a muddled affair, but in 1910 it was reorganised in a similar way to the French West African possessions and was renamed French Equatorial Africa.

While French West Africa consisted of eight territories, French Equatorial Africa was made up of four: Gabon, the Middle Congo, Oubangi Chari, and Chad. These territories stretch from the swamps of the Congo estuary right into the wastes of the Sahara, and some idea of their size is shown by the fact that Chad alone is twice as large as France. At first these areas, like the French West African ones, were supervised from France through a Governor-General in Brazzaville, who in turn supervised the Governors of each territory. One particularly interesting Governor was a Negro, Felix Eboué, who was Governor of Chad when France was defeated in Europe by Germany in 1940. Eboué at once refused to accept the rulers of the German government in France; instead he supported the Free French leader, General de Gaulle, whom we have already met in his later position as President. The other French Governors followed the example Eboué had set. This gave great advantages to the Allies who were fighting Germany. Another great character in this part of Africa is Dr Albert Schweitzer—perhaps the most famous European missionary in the continent—who has worked at Lambarene on the Ogowé River since 1913. When he decided to train as a doctor of medicine so that he could do this work he was already a famous organist, besides being a theologian and a philosopher.

The 1946 reorganisation was similar to that in West Africa: a Grand Council was set up representing the four territories, and in addition a Territorial Assembly was started in each region. When the French Community was established in 1958 the four territories remained within it and continued to be in it when they became independent in August 1960. The Middle Congo then became the Republic of the Congo and Oubangi Chari became the Central African Republic. These two, together with Chad, formed a Federation to deal with foreign affairs.

ECONOMIC AND SOCIAL DEVELOPMENT

Population

One of the most important differences between West Africa and other parts of Africa south of the Sahara is that West Africa has no settlers because its climate is unsuitable. This has made its constitutional and social development much simpler than in areas such as Kenya where there are a number of Indians and Europeans in addition to the African population.

Conditions of development

But, although there has been no settlement in West Africa, Europeans have been interested in its trade, and during this century West African trade has increased enormously. Subsistence farming still goes on, but a steadily increasing number of Africans have concentrated on growing crops for export. Increased exports have made it necessary to build ports where ships can dock and load instead of having to use surf boats; they have also made it necessary to build railways to carry the exports from the areas of production to the ports. As modern ports and railways are extremely expensive things to build, their construction has sometimes been delayed, and has always depended on the value of the territory's exports and the wealth of the European country with which the territory was connected. Ghana was able to develop rapidly because it had very valuable exports and because it had the support of Britain which is a wealthy country. Liberia, on the other hand, which had no direct connexions with any wealthy country and whose exports are small, had not even a railway line until 1951.

Agriculture

West Africa's wealth during this century has come chiefly from its agricultural exports, grown by African farmers often with only small areas of land. The products vary according to the climate and vegetation. The easiest regions to reach were the hot wet forests of the coast, and by a lucky chance it was these regions which produced the most valuable crops. Cocoa has been outstandingly successful. It was first brought to the Gold Coast in 1879 and in the first half of this century it came to produce well over half the colony's wealth. In recent years swollen shoot disease has somewhat reduced the cocoa export but it is still more valuable to Ghana than any other. Cocoa is not, of course, grown only in Ghana but has been developed in most of the coastal areas. Another major coastal product is palm oil, which has been an extremely important export from Nigeria since the nineteenth century. This, too, has been developed in other parts of the coast and notably in Dahomey and Sierra Leone. Valuable timber also comes from the forest lands.

Inland, where it becomes drier and the forests change to grassland and eventually to desert, other cash crops have been developed. The chief of these is ground-nuts which are produced in such huge quantities in the north of Nigeria that the railway has difficulty in transporting them all to the coast. In Gambia practically the whole wealth of the little territory depends on the export of ground-nuts.

Mining

As well as its agricultural products West Africa also has valuable minerals. Its gold first attracted Europeans to the coast in the fifteenth century and today gold is still a very important export, especially from Ghana where manganese, bauxite and diamonds are also found. In Nigeria the three chief minerals are tin and columbite from the north and coal from Enugu in the south. In Sierra Leone, minerals—especially diamonds and iron ore—provide more valuable exports than agriculture. The growth of mining in the French territories was not at first so rapid as in the British ones, but after the Second World War the French began to take a greater interest in minerals and in 1948 a special corporation was started to encourage mineral development. Today, mineral exports from these states are still small in comparison with those of agriculture, but Senegal produces titanium, Mauritania has big deposits of iron and copper, and French Equatorial Africa exports diamonds and lead. From the Republic of Guinea come iron, bauxite and diamonds.

There are many development schemes now under way in West Africa. One of the most interesting is the Volta River scheme which is expected to cost over £200 million. The plan is to build a barrage and hydro-electric station seventy miles from the mouth of the Volta River in Ghana. This will provide electric power on which the production of aluminium from bauxite ores near Kumasi depends. Besides bringing a great increase in wealth from the export of aluminium, the barrage will also create a huge lake which is expected to supply more fish each year than are at present caught in all the rest of Ghana.

Education

It would be very hard indeed to exaggerate the importance of education in the development of Africa south of the Sahara. In this respect West Africa has been lucky, because many parts of it have become rich enough to provide better educational opportunities than are available in other parts of the continent. The early schools and colleges were started by missionaries who saw the importance of education very clearly, but as expenses have increased the government has taken over the financing and much of the organisation of education. There have been some interesting landmarks in the educational advance in West Africa. The oldest African institution for higher education dates back to 1827 when Fourah Bay College in Sierra Leone was started by the Church Missionary Society and among its important ex-pupils is the present Prime Minister, Sir Milton Margai. The other colleges of West Africa were started in this century. Between the two World Wars there was much discussion about colonial education by the British government and one result of this was the starting of the Prince of Wales College at Achimota in 1929. One of the best-known names in connexion with this is Dr James Aggrey, the first vice-principal. This great Christian scholar was very wise, very tolerant and very cheerful. Once when he was travelling by boat, some of the European travellers refused to have their meals at his table because he was black; instead of being angry Aggrey simply smiled and observed how lucky he was to have the table all to himself while they were so crowded. He believed strongly in harmony between Africans and Europeans and one of his best known sayings was that 'in the harmony of the world as in the harmony of an organ or a piano, the black and white keys are both essential.' Through Achimota passed Dr Nkrumah and other leaders of Ghana. During the Second World War a special commission was appointed to encourage higher education in West Africa and as a result University Colleges were started in Ghana and at Ibadan in Nigeria in 1948. Today in West Africa—and anywhere else in the world for that matter—only a very small proportion of students ever reach university standard, but that does not mean that only a few attempt to reach it. In fact the demand for education in Africa is now so great that it is very difficult to provide enough schools and teachers.

In the French territories education developed more slowly. Greater attention was paid to it after the Second World War, however, and in the 1950's a University was started at Dakar which was similar in its standards to those of Ghana and Nigeria.

LIBERIA

Before leaving West Africa let us have a quick look at Liberia which has been an independent Republic for over a hundred years. It is ruled by a President who is assisted by a Cabinet, and there is a Senate and a House of Representatives. The government has been controlled by the immigrant Negroes of Monrovia, the capital, but since 1945 the Africans of the hinterland have also been represented.

However, the main problem of Liberia is not constitutional but economic. Liberia is desperately poor; much poorer than any of the other West African territories we have looked at. This is partly because other countries have been reluctant to invest money in the development of a small independent state with doubtful resources.

The chief export of Liberia for many years has been rubber, which has been mainly produced by the American Firestone Rubber plantations. Recently valuable deposits of iron ore have been found. Most of the outside help given to Liberia has come from the U.S.A., which financed the modern harbour of Monrovia in the late 1940's, and in 1950 started what was called the 'Point Four Plan' which gave financial and technical help. Nevertheless, education, transport, and a widespread African export trade are still sadly lacking.

CHAPTER 10

EAST AFRICA

The East African territories of Uganda, Kenya, Tanganyika and Zanzibar have each developed in different ways since the partition treaties of 1886 and 1890, and so we shall look at each separately.

UGANDA

We have already seen that Uganda officially became a British Protectorate in 1894. So far as the differences between the Protestant and Catholic parties were concerned, the years that followed were entirely peaceful because the new Roman Catholic Bishop appointed in 1895 was English. In other ways, however, Uganda still had its troubles. One of them was a rebellion by the Kabaka and his chiefs against the Protectorate's authority in 1897. This was fairly easily suppressed. More important was a mutiny, later in 1897, by the Sudanese soldiers upon whom the government relied, but by February of 1898 this too had been ended and peace restored.

The Uganda railway

The policy in Uganda was not just repression. Already, before the Sudanese mutiny began, a very positive step had been taken to develop the British East African territories. This was the construction of a railway from the port of Mombasa inland to Uganda. This had been suggested at the Brussels Conference in 1890, and was absolutely essential to the effective development of the interior, but there were serious obstacles. In the first place railways are very expensive, and there were men in the English Parliament who said that it would be wasting millions of pounds to build one in East Africa as there would be no goods to carry and so it would always run at a loss. They pointed out that the country was not properly mapped, that the African people knew nothing of railway building, and that the whole scheme was ridiculous. But in spite of their arguments the railway was built. In 1896 the first rails were laid from Mombasa, and by 1899 they had covered the 300 miles to the present site of Nairobi, despite the attacks of two lions in the Tsavo area. Most lions are lazy animals who much prefer animals to men as a meal. But the 'Man eaters of Tsavo' were an exception. They developed such a strong desire for human flesh that they leaped in and out of high stockades and took tremendous risks to get the food they wanted. So many men were taken and the rest were so terrified that work on the railway completely stopped for three weeks until the lions were shot. From the site of Nairobi the line climbed in and out of the Rift Valley and reached Kisumu on the shores of Lake Victoria in 1901. From there a boat, which had been carried from the coast in sections, brought goods across the lake to the northern shore near the capital, Kampala. It would be impossible to give too much importance to this railway, for upon it the development of Uganda and Kenya has depended. Nor did the railway affect only trade. It had very important social results as well, because its cheap transport finally ended the slave trade by making it unprofitable, and the speed and easiness of rail transport also made it possible for many more Indians and Europeans to enter the country than before.

The Uganda Agreement of 1900

While the railway was connecting the East African interior much more closely with the coast and the outside world, the British

Map 11. East Africa today.

attempted to reorganise Uganda which had become exhausted by the troubles of the previous years. The man sent as Consul-General was Sir Harry Johnston who had already been active in East, West and North Africa. By the 1900 agreement with the Kabaka, Buganda (which was the most important kingdom in the Protectorate) re-organised the system of landholding to give absolute ownership to individuals. The agreement also arranged that the Kabaka and his Lukiko (Parliament) should continue to rule Buganda with the approval of a British Commissioner or Governor—an arrangement which was very like that of Lugard's 'Indirect Rule' in Nigeria. Later agreements were made with other kingdoms in the Protectorate.

Constitutional development

Besides the agreements with each African kingdom, a central government was set up in 1902 for the whole Uganda Protectorate. At first this consisted of a Commissioner, whose title was changed to Governor in 1907, and in 1921 Executive and Legislative Councils were added.

We shall not follow the constitutional development of Buganda or the Uganda Protectorate step by step. There is the usual pattern of increasing representation, especially since 1945, leading towards responsible government. One crisis, however, should be mentioned which concerned the kingdom of Buganda. In 1953 the young Kabaka, who had recently returned from England after taking his degree at Cambridge University, found himself forced to choose between defying the wishes of his Lukiko or defying the wishes of the British Governor. He chose to defy the Governor and as a result he was deported to England where he spent a luxurious exile until new conditions were agreed upon which gave greater responsibility to the Lukiko ministers and recognised the Kabaka as a constitutional monarch like the English Queen, whose ministers—not herself—carried the responsibility for decisions of state. Then, in 1955, amid tremendous rejoicing, the Kabaka returned. To show their loyalty some of his subjects presented him with a cushion which was stuffed with the beards they had refused to shave until his return. While these changes were made in Buganda, representation of Africans in the Uganda Protectorate government was also greatly increased—three became ministers in the Executive Council and half the Legislative Council became African members. The process of giving more and more responsibility to African members and ministers has gone on, and the 1961 elections were planned on a non-racial basis, or common roll.

Since 1955 the policy of making Uganda more united has been encouraged by letting the people of each district elect their own representatives to the central Legislative Council. In the 1957 elections this happened in ten districts, and in the 1961 elections it was planned to happen everywhere, but the Kabaka of Buganda and his government feared that direct elections, and the policy of further uniting the Protectorate, might be harmful to the position and traditions of Buganda, so they instituted a boycott.

Today we may think of the Uganda Protectorate as a region with a central government consisting of a Governor, an Executive Council and a Legislative Council where all people from all parts of the Protectorate are represented. But within this region there are four African kingdoms—Buganda, Bunyoro, Ankole, Toro—in each of which there is a ruler assisted by Ministers and a Parliament to deal with local affairs. The rest of the Protectorate, besides these four kingdoms, is divided into districts where the local people are being given increasing responsibility in local government.

Economic and social development

Compared with the other East African territories Uganda is rich. At first this wealth came from cotton which was introduced in 1903–4 and has been carefully encouraged and controlled by the government. It is all grown by Africans on plots of land which vary from the size of a table-cloth to fields of several acres. In the early 1950's cotton exports alone brought in between £15 million and £30 million each year. In the late 1950's coffee, also grown by Africans, became as valuable as cotton. Mining has also been developed and in 1927 valuable copper deposits were found at Kilembe in the west and these became important when the railway reached them in 1956 through the railhead at Kasese.

Another great asset of Uganda is the Owen Falls Dam across the point where the Nile flows out of Lake Victoria. This was opened in 1954 and provides hydro-electric power, which has been used in Uganda and Kenya, and has encouraged the development of industries.

The social development of Uganda is different from that of Kenya, for Uganda has practically no European settlers. Out of a population of about six million there are about 9000 Europeans who are technicians or administrators—not landowners. The Asian population numbers about 50,000 and as usual they are particularly active in trade. In 1959 and 1960 some attempt was made by the Africans of Buganda to boycott their shops.

Uganda, like the other East African territories, has numerous primary and secondary schools. It also has at Kampala the University College of Makerere which was established in 1939 for students from all over East Africa.

KENYA

Until 1920 Kenya was known as British East Africa, and before 1900 it had hardly been touched by European influence. The Imperial British East Africa Company had established a few posts in the interior, and a band of missionaries had tried to start a station 150 miles inland at Kibwezi, but otherwise such administration as there was remained at the coast.

Settlement

Then came the railway and the picture began to change. Indian traders could now get inland where they began to develop trade, and the whole problem of communications was made easier. But in the opinion of Sir Charles Eliot, the Commissioner, what was really needed was a large number of European settlers to help develop the natural resources. It is interesting to notice that on this vital point he differed from Sir Hesketh Bell (the Commissioner of Uganda) who wanted Uganda to develop as an African state, a wish which was greatly helped by the success of African cotton growing. However, in Kenya Sir Charles Eliot decided to encourage European farmers to make the railway pay, and as the interior highlands were reasonably fertile and had a pleasant climate European settlement did in fact take place. But it was a slow business and even today the numbers, in comparison with the Rhodesias or the Union of South Africa, are small. As it happened, European settlement and farming did help to increase production and make the railway profitable, but at the same time it led to serious problems over land ownership, especially with the Kikuyu and Masai.

Lord Delamere

One European settler had by far the greatest influence in these early years—this was Lord Delamere, a wealthy red-headed English peer who gave up his rich estate in England in order to buy and develop a more exciting estate in the new colony. Some people thought him a wild, irresponsible man; on one occasion he drove a train off, leaving the Governor and his friends stranded in the bush; on another occasion he locked a hotel manager up all night in his meat safe for telling him it was time to leave. Other people admired his courage and determination, for he started by living very roughly in a hut and by losing a lot of money through unexpected difficulties from disease and wild animals. But by 1914 his worst struggles were over, and he had successfully established a wheat farm and a stock farm in the Rift Valley. His forceful character and his dislike of officialdom, together with his sacrificial efforts, made him the natural leader of the European settlers until his death in 1931.

It should not be thought, however, that Lord Delamere was the only person experimenting in agriculture at this time. While he concentrated on wheat and livestock, others were experimenting successfully with the growing of coffee, tea, sisal and fruit.

The Devonshire White Paper, 1923

The early period of settlement and agricultural experiment was followed by the 1914–18 war, after which the European community was given greater representation in the government. This led straight to trouble with the Indian community who also demanded representation and the right to own land in the highlands. The agitation lasted for three years, and in the final settlement of 1923, known as the Devonshire White Paper, a very important statement was made to the effect that in all questions the interests of the African population should be regarded as supremely important. Although this did not cause exceptional excitement in Kenya it did alarm European settlers in the Rhodesias. More recently the British Government has inclined towards the policy of upholding the rights of all people who have made their homes in Kenya.

The Mau Mau rebellion

There is not space to discuss all the troubles of the next thirty years, but the Mau Mau rebellion in the early 1950's by some of the Kikuyu tribe against the government needs a mention. It was anti-European, anti-Christian, and very interested in the land question. For several years the rebellion kept the highland area of Kenya in a state of unrest, for the gangs of terrorists who hid in the thick forests of the Aberdare Mountains were extremely difficult to catch. But the rebellion was a local affair, and in some ways it was like a civil war, for many Kikuyu rejected it altogether and supported the government, and most of the people killed were Kikuyu loyalists. By 1955 the worst was over. Unfortunately, however, Kenya was not rich enough to afford rebellion on any scale, and its economic development was hindered and once more loans from Britain became necessary. Some interesting and useful changes were, however, made as a result; one was the gathering together of separate family settlements into large villages; another was the process of land consolidation by which scattered plots of land were re-arranged to give each African land-holder one compact area which could be more easily worked than the separate ones.

General development

Apart from the upheaval caused by Mau Mau, during the last thirty years Kenya has made great progress. Its trade, its agriculture, its industries, its hospitals and its education have all developed rapidly, especially since the end of the Second World War. To help with higher education the Royal Technical College—now called the Royal College—was opened in Nairobi in 1956.

Nairobi and the High Commission

Although the main port of East Africa is Mombasa, the capital of Kenya is Nairobi which lies about 300 miles inland. At the start of the century it was a frog-infested swamp; today it is the main commercial centre of the East African territories. Among other modern buildings in the city is that of the High Commission, which was started in 1948 to deal with services which affect all the East African territories such as the post office, the railways and agricultural research. It is assisted by the East African Central Legislative Assembly.

Constitutional development

The constitutional development of Kenya has been complicated because of the European and Indian populations there. Although an Executive Council was started in 1905 and a Legislative Council in 1907, there were at first no elected members at all and Lord Delamere walked out of the Legislative Council because he thought it was useless except to give consent to the Governor's plans. After the 1914–18 war the position changed. Unofficial Europeans were appointed to the Executive Council and elected Europeans entered the Legislative; so did Indian representatives after some fierce disputes. Africans at first were represented by special members owing to language difficulties, but as education developed more and more Africans took part in the government. The first African representative entered the Legislative Council in 1944 and since then the proportion of African representation has increased continually. A big step forward was made in 1954 when a Council of Ministers was established including Africans, Europeans and Indians, which took over the Executive Council's task of advising the Governor. In 1960, at the Lancaster House Conference in London attended by the leaders of all races, still greater advances were planned. The franchise was widened considerably for the 1961 elections to give Africans a majority in the enlarged Legislative Council. For the first time an African became leader of Government business in the Council. Though the Governor retained many of his powers, in particular the right to nominate members to ensure a Government majority, the way was opened to the appointment of an African Chief Minister and, in due course, full self-government.

Racial position

Of the four main races in Kenya today the Africans easily outnumber the rest; probably there are about seven million. Increasing numbers of them are taking responsibility not only in politics but also in the main professions and business concerns. The next most numerous group are the Indians who number about 170,000 and manage most of the petty trade, and then come the Europeans who number about 60,000 and include farmers, government officials, business men and missionaries. Most of the 36,000 Arabs are found at the coast.

TANGANYIKA

Uganda, Kenya and Zanzibar have been connected with Britain since the Partitition Treaties of 1886 and 1890, but Tanganyika's connexions with Britain did not begin until 1918. Before that it was known as German East Africa and was administered first by a Company and from 1891, after the Arab rebellion, by the German government.

German administration

The German administration had some good points—it started an excellent research station at Amani and made great efforts with education—but it was not popular. Except in Ruanda, Urundi and Bukoba it ignored the existing tribal leaders and replaced them with German, Arab and Swahili administrators who were often of poor quality. They were much disliked. The question of settlement and labour also caused ill-feeling, for the Germans, like the British in Kenya, thought that the best way to develop the resources of the country was to encourage European settlement, and so German farmers began to buy and farm land in the northern highlands at Moshi and Arusha, and on the coast at Tanga and Pangani. The African people resented these land grants and the forced labour which they were compelled to give. To add to the discontent there was the usual hut tax, and taxation has never been popular anywhere.

Rebellions

The African people showed their dislike in a series of rebellions starting with the Hehe in 1891. But by far the worst was the Maji-Maji rebellion (1905–7) when the tribes of the south joined together in an attempt to drive out the Germans. They failed, but it was easily the greatest rebellion East Africa has seen, and by the time it ended about 100,000 Africans and many Europeans had died or been killed, and much of the land in the south was ruined. As similar rebellions had occurred at about the same time in the Cameroons and South West Africa the German government tried to improve their administration and give more encouragement to African production, but these efforts were not very effective because the settlers opposed them.

Economic development

The Germans never made a profit from their colony, but nevertheless considerable economic progress was made. The main crop was sisal which had been introduced in 1893, and coffee, cotton, and ground-nuts had also been found suitable. Meanwhile two railway lines had been built: the Usambara railway in the north, and the Central Line further south which was completed in 1914.

The 1914–18 war

The war which broke out in Europe in 1914, between Britain and France on one side and Germany on the other, need not have affected Africa, but in fact it did, and all the German colonies were captured. Usually this was a quick business, but in East Africa it was not, because the Germans there happened to have an outstanding leader in Von Lettow Vorbeck, and although a big attack was made upon his comparatively small army in 1916 he held out until the final peace was signed in Europe in 1918. The war in East Africa was a tragedy. It wasted tens of thousands of lives, it wasted millions of pounds of money, and it laid waste large areas of the country. Tanganyika looked as though it could never recover.

The British mandate

But it did recover, and remarkably quickly too. By the peace treaty made in Europe, German East Africa (except for Ruanda and Urundi which went to Belgium) was put in the care of Britain as a 'mandate' so that its affairs were supervised by the League of Nations. It was then renamed 'Tanganyika'. By 1923 it no longer needed financial aid, and in 1925 it began to be reorganised when Sir Donald Cameron became its Governor. Sir Donald Cameron had spent a while as an official in Nigeria under Lord Lugard, and there he had seen the policy of 'indirect rule' in action. When he became Governor of Tanganyika he took the opposite policy to that of the Germans. Instead of setting aside the authority of the African chiefs he did his best to restore it by seeking out in each area chiefs who would really be acknowledged by the African people. He was very successful, and the African authorities which he set up were given wide responsibilities including judicial powers and the collection of taxes.

Constitutional development

While local government was reorganised the central government was developed also, and in 1926 a Legislative Council was introduced. As usual, the members at first were all nominated, and the first elections were not held until 1958. From that time changes have been rapid and peaceful. In 1959 a Council of Ministers was set up as the Governor's advisers, and the 1960 elections gave the elected members a majority in the Legislative Council with the African leader of the majority party, Mr Nyerere, acting as chief minister. At the end of 1961 Tanganyika became fully independent.

Social and economic development

Tanganyika, as we might expect from its greater size, has the largest population of all the East African territories. There are about eight million Africans of over 100 different tribes mostly of Bantu origin. There are also about 75,000 Indians and about 20,000 Europeans who are now mainly British and Greeks.

Most of the African population live on the highlands, the lakeside or on the coastal plain where they graze their cattle, cultivate their land and hope to produce enough food for themselves besides a small cash crop of cotton, coffee or ground-nuts. It has been the general policy of the government to increase the general wealth of the territory by encouraging African farmers, and exports of their crops have risen steadily. However, there has been no deliberate exclusion of settlers and the wealth of both Europeans and Indians has helped Tanganyika greatly, especially by building up the sisal industry which provides the most valuable part of Tanganyika's exports. The discovery of the Williamson diamond mine at Shinyanga in 1940 has also greatly helped the territory's prosperity.

ZANZIBAR

We have seen that the neighbouring islands of Zanzibar and Pemba became a British Protectorate by the Heligoland Treaty of 1890. By that time the importance of Zanzibar was already over because the treaties made between Britain and Germany had divided the mainland into spheres of influence over which the Sultan no longer had any control, and from which he no longer obtained the profits of trade. As the mainland territories developed, with their harbours at Mombasa and Dar es Salaam, Zanzibar ceased to be the main commercial centre and became more of a unit on its own.

The early years of the Zanzibar Protectorate were not happy ones. The people and government of England had little sympathy because of Zanzibar's reputation as a slave market, and in addition they thought that the Sultan's administration needed to be greatly improved to end corruption. The alterations, restrictions, and demands made by the British—and especially the demand that Zanzibar should pay £200,000 compensation to IBEA—led to a rebellion in 1895. This was suppressed, but in the next year further trouble occurred when Sultan Hamed died and his succession was disputed, but after a quick bombardment Sultan Hamoud, whom the British had nominated, was established.

During Sultan Hamoud's reign, in 1897, slavery was officially ended in Zanzibar. It had been feared that this would ruin the clove industry, but in fact clove production increased. It had also been expected that there would be great excitement among the slaves but in fact there was not because on the whole they were not badly treated. Many did not even bother to claim their freedom.

The five short reigns after the death of Sultan Barghash in 1888 were followed by the very long reign of Khalifa II who became Sultan in 1911 and reigned until 1960—a kindly Arab aristocrat whose bright red car became a familiar sight along the roads between the swishing green palms of his island.

In 1913 the supervision of Zanzibar's administration was transferred from the Foreign Office to the Colonial Office, and a Protectorate Council was started, but in 1925 this was abolished and the usual Executive and Legislative Councils were set up. In 1956 a Privy Council was also started to advise the Sultan and the other councils were enlarged. The first general elections were held in 1957, and in 1960 it was recommended that the Legislative Council should have a majority of elected members. It was also suggested that the Executive Council should be reorganised so that its president (the British Resident) could ask the leader of the majority party to become chief minister and choose four colleagues as the basis of his government. This would mean that the Executive Council would probably become a Council of Ministers.

Economic and social development

From the air the island of Zanzibar looks like an almost solid mass of palm trees, but the coconut industry is only second in importance in Zanzibar's economy. The greatest export is that of cloves, and of these Zanzibar and Pemba produce most of the world's supply.

The money from these products has been used in several ways to improve conditions on the island. Livingstone's name for it was 'Stinkibar' because of the smell and the dirt which were to be found in the narrow streets. Today the narrow streets are still there in Zanzibar, but there are new wide ones as well which are swept and clean. Nearly 300 miles of tarmac roads join the various parts of the island, and there have been steady improvements in schools and hospitals.

Most of the population are Africans (230,000), next come the Arabs (47,000) and there are also about 19,000 Indians. Although Europeans play an important part in the administration of the island there are only about 500 of them altogether.

CHAPTER 11

CENTRAL AFRICA

In this chapter we shall be looking at the territories of Southern Rhodesia, Northern Rhodesia and Nyasaland.

SOUTHERN RHODESIA

We have already seen that settlement in Southern Rhodesia was started by Rhodes' South Africa Company in 1890 when the pioneers marched into Fort Salisbury. At first the areas of the Company's activity were known as Northern and Southern Zambezia, but in 1895, to Rhodes' great delight, they were officially named Rhodesia. Southern Rhodesia, which was made up of Mashonaland and Matabeleland, was the region to the south of the Zambezi; Northern Rhodesia was the region to the north of the river.

Rhodes' idea had been that Rhodesia should become self-governing and an extra province of South Africa, but things did not work out exactly as he had planned. For the first part of its history Southern Rhodesia was controlled by the South Africa Company whose chief official was called the Administrator, and this was the position which Dr Jameson held until the disastrous Jameson Raid. Almost from the outset there was also a Legislative Council and by 1914 this had a majority of elected members.

In this year the Company's charter ended, as it had been granted for only twenty-five years from 1889. The settlers were then given the choice of having the Company's charter renewed or joining with the Union of South Africa as Rhodes had expected. The Company's administration was not particularly popular, but on the other hand the settlers were alarmed by the Afrikaner element in the Union and by the outbreak of the 1914–18 World War. Therefore, they decided to renew the Company's charter for another ten years.

During those years several suggestions were made about the future. One suggestion, made by the Chairman of the Company, was that Southern Rhodesia should unite with Northern Rhodesia. This was definitely rejected by the settlers who felt that the north was far less developed and might hold back the south. Another suggestion was that Southern Rhodesia should unite with the Union as another province. General Smuts, the Union's Prime Minister, was very keen to encourage this, and he offered such generous conditions and the economic advantages—such as the use of the Union's ports— were so obvious that many settlers thought that joining the Union would be the best policy. A third suggestion was that Southern Rhodesia should become a British colony with responsible government. In 1922 the settlers of Southern Rhodesia were given the chance to choose which alternative they preferred. They decided, by 8774 votes to 5989, to become a self-governing British colony. And so the South Africa Company's rule of Southern Rhodesia ended,

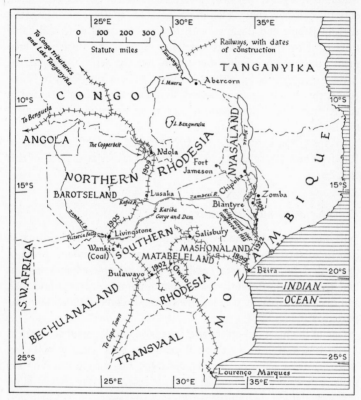

Map 12. Central Africa today.

although it continued to control all mineral rights until 1933, and all railways until 1945, while its trading affairs still continue today.

But so far as the government of Southern Rhodesia was concerned the Company's administration was finished. Instead, a new constitution arranged for a Governor assisted by an Executive Council and an elected Legislative Assembly. As the Governor's Ministers were the chosen leaders of the elected Legislative Assembly Southern Rhodesia did get responsible government. But it did not become an entirely self-governing Dominion because affairs concerning the African people and dealings with foreign countries were still liable to control by the British government. One of the British government's reasons for keeping this control was the desire to protect the African population, for although voting was not restricted to Europeans, the qualifications necessary to obtain a vote have resulted in the African population being a very small proportion of the electorate.

In 1953 Southern Rhodesia became part of the Federation of Rhodesia and Nyasaland, which we shall consider at the end of this chapter.

Economic and social development

Rhodes hoped that the areas his Company opened might prove as rich in minerals as the Transvaal. He was disappointed. Most of the settlers became farmers, and the most valuable exports were at first agricultural. Recently the mining of chrome, asbestos and coal, and the development of industries have become increasingly important.

One of the most important and expensive development schemes in Africa was started in Southern Rhodesia in 1955 when work began on the Kariba Dam on the Zambezi 300 miles from the Victoria Falls. The dam was opened in 1960. It cost well over £100 million and is the largest dam in the world, towering over 400 feet high and creating a lake 200 miles long. It should provide almost unlimited hydro-electric power for the development of industries in the Federation, and will be especially useful for the copper-belt of Northern Rhodesia.

Both the Rhodesias and Nyasaland have been handicapped in their development because they have no coastline. From the beginning Rhodes and the South Africa Company tried to overcome this by the rapid building of railways. As the Transvaal government would not allow the line from the Cape to Kimberley to be continued northwards through their territory, Rhodes took it instead through Bechuanaland. By 1891 it reached Vryburg, by 1902 it reached Bulawayo and Salisbury, and a line was also built northwestwards through Northern Rhodesia to join the Congo railway. Meanwhile, in 1899, the Southern Rhodesian line was also connected to the Portuguese port of Beira in Mozambique. Today the hinterland which Beira serves is enormous.

Socially, Southern Rhodesia has a large white settler population of over 200,000 (compared with the 70,000 settlers of Northern Rhodesia and the 60,000 of Kenya), but they are outnumbered by ten to one in comparison with the African population of two and a half million. The main African tribes are the Matabele in the south and the Mashona to the north. Racial separation is not so strict as it is in the Union, but on the other hand it is much stricter than in the East African territories.

The Rhodesias and Nyasaland at first sent African students who qualified for higher education to universities in the Union of South Africa, but in the early 1950's the idea of building a University College at Salisbury was hurried on. This was taken over by the Federal Government, and in 1955 the Queen Mother accepted its Presidency.

NORTHERN RHODESIA

Northern Rhodesia is a Protectorate. It is twice as large as Southern Rhodesia but it has fewer people (two and a quarter million Africans and 70,000 Europeans) and has only developed rapidly in the last thirty years. One example of the speed of change has been the development of the Northern Rhodesian capital Lusaka. In 1954 an American visitor described it as looking like a Wild West scene from the films. Five years later it looked as modern as any town in Africa.

Constitutional development

At first the region north of the Zambezi fell into three divisions. One was the Barotseland Protectorate in the west which began in 1890 when the Barotse chief, Lewanika, asked the Queen for British protection against the Matabele. This Protectorate still exists. The other two divisions were the North-West and North-East Provinces which were united with the title of Northern Rhodesia in 1911. Until 1924 this area of Northern Rhodesia was administered by the South Africa Company through an Administrator who was assisted from 1918 by an Advisory Council. In 1924 the British government took over the administration, and Northern Rhodesia was given the usual constitution with a Governor plus an Executive Council and Legislative Council. These councils have since been enlarged, and by the 1959 constitution African ministers were included in the Executive. As the government must also pay attention to the wishes of the leader of the majority party in the Legislative Council, Northern Rhodesia has gone some way towards responsible government.

Economic and social development

The most striking part of Northern Rhodesia's history is its economic development during the last thirty years. When the South Africa Company entered this area of savanna and bush, they hoped it would prove fertile, but they were disappointed. By 1914 the few settlers who had taken up land were mainly beside the railway line or around Fort Jameson or Abercorn. Most of them were ranchers and traders, and the main crops were maize, cotton and tobacco. The African population, except in the more fertile areas such as the Barotse plain, found the soil so poor that they had to keep moving from one area to another in order to grow crops, while the tsetse fly prevented cattle-keeping in many districts. It is not therefore surprising that in 1914 Southern Rhodesia feared, among other things, that union with Northern Rhodesia would be an economic burden and rejected the idea.

But in the thirty years since then the picture has completely changed. Northern Rhodesia has become rich, and the product which has made her rich is copper. About £90 million of it are sold each year and it provides over 90 % of Northern Rhodesia's exports. The area from which this wealth comes is the copper belt, which lies just south of Katanga in the Congo. Although copper was known to exist in the area in 1899 it was not until 1927 that the 'Roan Antelope' mine opened, to be followed by others, and the great copper boom began. Today, Northern Rhodesia has the greatest copper-producing industry in the world after those of the United States of America and Chile. Until the opening of the Kariba Dam in 1960, one of the great problems of the copper belt was that of obtaining fuel for the furnaces, but now hydro-electric power should provide all that is needed.

Although the wealth of Northern Rhodesia comes from its minerals most of the Africans in the Protectorate are farmers, and the main crop is maize. The African population includes over seventy different tribes, the chief of whom are the Barotse. The Makololo, from whom came Livingstone's most loved and faithful helpers, are also of Northern Rhodesia. The European population are mostly town dwellers, but there are some farmers, mainly in the south and central provinces.

NYASALAND

Nyasaland is much smaller than either of the Rhodesias but it contains the largest African population (2,700,000 compared with 2,400,000 in Southern Rhodesia).

Its constitutional history until 1953, when it became part of the Federation, may be briefly told. We have already seen that in 1891 it was officially claimed by the British as the British Central African Protectorate. In 1907 it was renamed Nyasaland and received a new constitution of the usual sort—a Governor, plus an Executive and Legislative Council, whose representative membership was increased from time to time. Meanwhile, District Councils were started in most of the districts in Nyasaland to enable the African people to share in local government.

Economically Nyasaland has not made such an impressive advance as the Rhodesias, but nevertheless its exports have very considerably increased, especially since the Second World War. The main export crops which have been developed are tobacco, tea and cotton, but the total exports are small by world standards; fishing, forestry and factories of several kinds are also developing. Generally, Nyasaland is a territory of peasant farmers, herdsmen, and fishermen. One of the big problems of development has been communications, which were made more difficult by the fall in the level of the Shiré River. To provide an outlet for Nyasaland's exports the Shiré Highlands Railway was started in 1904 to connect the highlands with the northern bank of the Zambezi. In 1922 a railway was built from the southern bank to Beira, and in 1935 a bridge across the river was built to provide continuous rail communication. The northern end was later extended to the shore of the lake itself.

Unlike the Rhodesias, Nyasaland has only a very small number of settlers—less than 1 % of the total population. In the 1880's some claims to land were made by the South Africa Company and others, but today only 5 % of the land is alienated, and most of this is in the control of Companies and not individual settlers. On the whole the relations between the Africans and Europeans in Nyasaland have been very friendly. Today the Yao and Angoni are among the chief tribes, but there are many others.

THE CENTRAL AFRICAN FEDERATION

We have seen that Southern Rhodesia is a colony which has had responsible government since 1923, and that Northern Rhodesia and Nyasaland are Protectorates. The idea of uniting some, or all, of them was first put forward by Dr Jameson in 1915 when he suggested that the Rhodesias should unite. The idea was then rejected, but during the next twenty years Europeans in Northern and Southern Rhodesia became more interested in the possibilities of amalgamation. This was partly due to the economic benefits it would bring, and partly because it was hoped that amalgamation would give the Rhodesias the status of a Dominion with no control from the British government, which had caused alarm in 1923 by declaring in the Devonshire White Paper in connexion with Kenya (see p. 116) that African interests should be given priority over those of settlers. As a result of the interest in amalgamation a Royal Commission led by Lord Bledisloe was appointed in 1937 to investigate the possibilities of closer union between the Rhodesias and Nyasaland. Its advice was clear: closer union might be desirable later but not at once, because the differences between the three territories were thought to be too great. But the Commission did suggest that a Council, which represented all three territories, should be started to help co-operation and, as a result, in 1945 after the Second World War the Central African Council was set up. However, this was only advisory.

In 1951 a further conference was held in London to consider union. On one side it was argued that some kind of union would avoid the possibility of Southern Rhodesia's joining the Union of South Africa (whose policy of 'apartheid' alarmed many people), and that it would bring advantages in economic development and administration. On the other side it was argued that the largest number of Europeans were in Southern Rhodesia which was therefore likely to prove the greatest political influence. This the Africans greatly feared. The decision of the conference was that a Federation should be established in which each territory kept its government and control of its own affairs, but in addition a Federal Assembly was started with African and European representatives from Southern Rhodesia, Northern Rhodesia and Nyasaland. This assembly could deal with foreign affairs, customs, communications and other general matters. It could not interfere in local affairs in any one territory. The Federation scheme also stated that the rights and advancement of the African people should be cared for.

This decision was supported by most of the European population in the Rhodesias. Most of the African population, however, opposed it. Nevertheless, in 1953 the Federation came into being, and it was hoped that it would improve race relations by bringing benefits to all.

In fact it has aroused opposition as well as support. Dr Hastings Banda of Nyasaland wants his country to leave the Federation, while Sir Roy Welensky, the Federation's 20-stone Prime Minister who worked his way up from being a bare-fist boxer and trade-union leader, is determined that the Federation shall remain intact. The Monckton Commission, which investigated the Federation's affairs in 1960, did not advise breaking the federal association but it did suggest immediate political advances and the ending of all forms of racial discrimination.

The Asian population in the Federation

Although the main groups in the Federation are the Africans and Europeans, there is also an Asian population in each which in 1960 numbered 14,000 in Southern Rhodesia, 8000 in Northern Rhodesia and 11,000 in Nyasaland. As in East Africa, they are mostly shop-keepers and business men. In 1954, after the formation of the Federation, the Federal government forbade, with some exceptions, any further Asian immigration.

CHAPTER 12

THE CONGO, ANGOLA AND MOZAMBIQUE

THE CONGO

The chief reforms which Leopold of the Belgians had promised to carry out when he was recognised as ruler of the Congo Free State were the civilising of the country and the abolition of the slave trade there.

At first it looked as though these reforms were being honestly attempted because a war against the Arab slavers started in 1892. These slavers came from the east coast and had reached the Upper Congo in the early nineteenth century. In time they became the chief influence there and major slaving centres were established at Nyangwe and Kasongo. Tippoo Tib, who was the most important of the slavers, was actually made Governor of the region for Leopold from 1887 to 1890 in the hope that he would preserve peace there. The Arabs, however, had always been hostile to a European administration which opposed their slaving, and as Belgian control of the Congo grew stronger they decided to make an attempt to keep the Upper Congo for themselves before it was too late. The Arab rebellion in East Africa against the Germans, and the export duty on ivory exported from the Congo, spurred them on. Therefore, in 1892, the Arabs attacked and killed Belgian administrators and traders in the Upper Congo. At once a force of European and African troops advanced against them, and in one of the most exciting military campaigns in African history the Arab strongholds of Nyangwe and Kasongo were taken and destroyed. As a result, by 1894, Arabs no longer controlled the Upper Congo, and the slave trade which had gone on in the region came to an end.

But apart from this successful campaign, Leopold's rule was disastrous. His wealth was nothing like so great as that of a colonising power like Britain, and lacking wealth he had to face the problem of making his huge state pay for its development. This led straight to a policy of strict trade control and to frightening and exceptional cruelty. After the Berlin Congress it was expected that the administration and trade of the Congo state would be shared by the countries of Europe. For a few years they were, but by the early 1890's the administration of the state was almost entirely in Belgian hands, and the very profitable trade in ivory and rubber had become, except in the coastal region, a strict monopoly of special companies appointed and controlled by the king. In 1896 Leopold took for himself 100,000 square miles of the Congo as his private estate. The ivory and rubber were obtained by forcing the Congo people

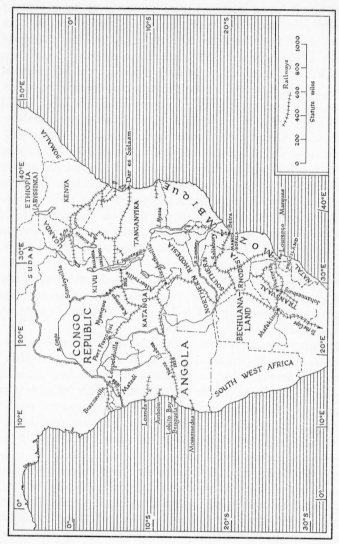

Map 13. The Congo, Angola and Mozambique.

to produce fixed amounts which were collected by African overseers who were authorised to cut the hands off, or shoot, defaulters. These brutal methods greatly reduced the population. They also horrified the people of Europe when the true facts became known.

The man who was chiefly responsible for publicising the facts was a young British shipping clerk called Morel. At first nobody would believe him because it seemed impossible that the noble, well-dressed Leopold, who seemed so polite and pleasant, could possibly permit such atrocities. But when a special commission was sent in 1904 and found that Morel's facts were correct, there could no longer be any doubt, and in 1908 the Congo ceased to be governed by Leopold himself, and was handed over to be administered by the Belgian government. There is not much that can or should be said in Leopold's defence, but perhaps it should be added that he himself never visited the Congo to see the suffering there. Also, some areas of the Congo in the north and east were not affected by his concession companies, and on the main travelling routes there were already signs of improved agriculture and considerable missionary activity.

Constitutional development

When the Belgian government took over the administration of the Congo it was mainly interested in ending the abuses which had taken place during Leopold's rule, and in developing the general prosperity of the country.

The basic law for the Congo state was laid down in the Colonial Charter of 1908. By this Charter the control of the Congo was placed in the hands of the King of Belgium and the Parliament of Belgium. It also created a Minister for the Colonies and a Colonial Council whose work was to consider and advise on all laws concerning the Congo.

In the Congo itself a Governor-General, responsible to the Minister in Belgium, was made the head of the administration. In 1914 a Government Council was created consisting of nominated members whose duty was to assist the Governor-General with advice. In 1947, after the Second World War, further changes were made. A Vice-Governor-General was added and the Government Council was increased to include thirty unofficial members as well as officials. By 1951 the unofficials included eight Africans. But all members of the Government Council were nominated, not elected, and no African or European had a vote. The state was controlled as a family with a strong father might be controlled, and to all appearances there was prosperity and political quiet.

But in January of 1959 the scene began to change at a tremendous speed when a political meeting of the ABAKO party in Dendale (the African suburb of Leopoldville) turned into a riot. Shops were burnt and a number of people were killed before order was restored. The Belgian King Baudouin and his government held meetings with the political leaders, and after various negotiations it was agreed that the Congo should become independent at the end of June 1960. This was a much more rapid constitutional change than had taken place elsewhere in Africa. The immediate results were sad. Within a few days of independence the Congo army mutinied, many Europeans fled, and troops of the United Nations were flown in to restore order and to help. Meanwhile, some of the provinces—including the vital copper-producing region of Katanga—claimed their independence from the central government and asked that the Congo should become a Federation. Many died as starvation and violence spread through the country. Prime Minister Lumumba was killed, and while attempts were made to form a government such authority as there was depended mainly on the United Nations.

Economic development

From the outset the Belgians thought it was more important to develop the prosperity of the Congo rather than its political arrangements; to provide wealth before votes. It was therefore on the economic side that—until 1960—the greatest advances were made.

Economic development in the Congo was mainly encouraged by a few very large companies with which the Belgian government was closely concerned. These were very different from the early monopoly companies of Leopold. Besides training the Africans they employed, they also provided houses in carefully planned villages with free food, free clothing, and wages of sometimes £35 a month.

The first main exports of the Congo were rubber and ivory, but now the main agricultural items are cotton and coffee. The Congo's economic development, however, has certainly not depended only on her agricultural resources, for the Belgians have always regarded the minerals of the Congo as particularly important. The chief of these is copper, which was discovered in the Katanga region in 1891, and today the Katanga district, with its centre at Elisabethville, is the most important mining area in the Congo.

One of the greatest problems the Belgians had to face was that of reaching the productive regions, for although it was realised that the potential wealth of the Congo was huge, so was its size. The chief means of transport was—and still is—the Congo River itself, which is navigable for most, but not all, of its length. Railways were therefore needed to cover the unnavigable stretches, and to connect the main production centres with the river; these are shown on map 13.

To speed up the economic development of the Congo in 1949 the Belgians published a Ten Year Plan, costing £350 million. This helped considerably in developing communications and improving living conditions in the towns. After the Second World War the Belgians also started a special Welfare Fund to help the African peasants by improving health services and education.

Social development

At the start of 1960 the Congo had about thirteen million Africans and about 100,000 Europeans.

The African population has over 200 tribes. Probably the best-known people are the Pygmies, who live in the thick, dark forest of the north-east on the Uganda border, and the Baluba, whose king traces his ancestry back through three centuries. According to custom the Baluba king must have one wife for every pound of his weight; a recent king is said to have weighed 250 lb. and had 250 wives.

The health and education of the Congo people were pioneered—as in other parts of Africa—by the missions, who have been increasingly helped by the state. The first missionary society to establish missions along the Congo was that of the Baptist Church, but most of the Belgians are Roman Catholics and since 1906 the Catholic missions have been by far the greatest influence. In addition to their evangelistic work, which has brought over two million of the Congo people into the Christian church, they have guided the educational policy, which has emphasised practical and technical matters rather than advanced academic knowledge. However, in 1954, a University College was opened at Lovanium near Leopoldville, and a few years later another was started at Elisabethville.

The Belgian rulers did not wish for a strict colour bar in the Congo. Africans were found in skilled work in the mines, in industry, on the railways, and as teachers and administrators. But some distinctions were made. For example, Leopoldville consisted of two cities—an African and a European—although these were not strictly separated except at night.

The European population is mostly Belgian and most are employed in administrative work and as directors of the companies, mines and industries. There are very few individual European settlers who own land, except in the Kivu district where the climate is most suitable. Big land grants have, however, been made to companies.

RUANDA-URUNDI

After the First World War the two African kingdoms of Ruanda and Urundi, which had been part of German East Africa, became a mandate of the League of Nations administered by the Belgians. After the Second World War they became a trust territory of the United Nations and remained in Belgian hands.

They are administered in the same way as was the Congo with

some important exceptions. Ruanda and Urundi each have a king, or sultan, who is called a 'Mwami' and has a similar position to that of the Kabaka of Uganda. He is assisted by chiefs and subchiefs. There is also a Belgian Resident who advises the Mwami. The official head of the united territory of Ruanda-Urundi is a Belgian Governor who is assisted by an advisory council which includes African members.

The dominant Ruanda tribe are the Watutsi. Their ancestors probably arrived in the region about 500 years ago, and their descendants have remained the ruling class. They are remarkable, among other things, for their height. The present Mwami Kigeri V —an educated Roman Catholic who speaks fluent French—is 6 feet 9 inches tall. Some of his subjects are well over 7 feet.

Like the Congo, Ruanda-Urundi will achieve independence in the near future. In 1959 this prospect caused a serious revolt in Ruanda when the Bahutu rebelled against the Watutsi, causing considerable loss of life before peace was restored.

Ruanda-Urundi has developed as an agricultural country. The European population is very small, and settlement has only been allowed in special cases.

THE PORTUGUESE OVERSEAS PROVINCES

The partition of Africa ended Portuguese hopes of gaining control over a continuous belt of territory stretching from Angola in the west to Mozambique in the east. By the 1891 agreement it had been recognised that the British possession of Rhodesia lay like a barrier between the Portuguese possessions on the Atlantic and Indian oceans. For about ten years after the 1891 agreement it looked as though the Portuguese coastal possessions might also be lost because Portugal was so weak in comparison with Britain, Germany and France, but in fact the Portuguese held on.

In the twentieth century the story of Portugal's overseas possessions has been so closely connected with home affairs that we shall look first at Portugal itself.

In 1910, after a short revolution, the Portuguese deposed their king and established a Republic instead. At first it seemed as if this would lead to reforms and greater efficiency in the overseas territories. Actually it led to a policy of giving more responsibility to the Governors of each territory and less to the Portuguese government at home. This policy was not a success, and the colonies got into serious debt. As a result, when a new Portuguese government came into power in 1926 the policy was changed, and the Portuguese overseas territories were brought under closer supervision from Portugal. This has especially been the case since the quietly efficient Dr Salazar, professor of law, became Prime Minister in 1932. In 1951 Portuguese territories in Africa were officially called 'Overseas Provinces' which were to be administered like parts of Portugal itself. At the same time the name of the Ministry of the Colonies was changed to that of the Ministry for Overseas Provinces, and all the people in the provinces were ranked as Portuguese citizens who could vote in Portuguese elections. Thus, Angola and Mozambique both elect three Deputies to the National Assembly in Portugal.

The real political power in Portugal itself, however, rests not with the National Assembly but with the Council of State led by the Prime Minister. One of the members of this Council is the Minister for Overseas Provinces, who is responsible for legislation and all matters concerning Portuguese overseas possessions. To make sure that its laws are obeyed the Ministry has Inspectors whose only task is to report on the administration of the provinces.

The central government of Mozambique and Angola is in the hands of Governors-General. Since 1926 they have been assisted by Councils of Government, and in 1955 Legislative Councils were organised. The powers of these Councils are very limited, however. Besides the central government, there are also local government units, in the smaller of which African chiefs take part.

A feature of Portuguese administration is the official refusal to recognise any colour bar. From the earliest days of Portuguese colonisation, marriages between Africans and Europeans have been readily accepted. This still applies, and the children of such marriages have full rights as citizens. Moreover, no shops, hotels, or trades are closed to Africans for racial reasons. But there is a very important distinction which the Portuguese do make and that is between Portuguese citizens and Portuguese natives. All Europeans are automatically 'citizens'. All Africans are automatically 'natives', unless they pass special tests and so pass into the 'citizen' class. It is very difficult, but not impossible, to rise from one class to another and at present the number of African citizens is very small in comparison with the total population, but in theory the Portuguese hope that all Africans will eventually be citizens.

Economically Portugal is not a wealthy country, but since 1935 her overseas territories have not run at a loss. Moreover, there have been a series of National Development Schemes whose funds have been divided about equally between improvements in Portugal and improvements to her overseas provinces.

But despite recent improvements, in the early years of the century the rate of development of Portuguese territories in Africa was much slower than in most other regions and that lag has not yet been made up.

Now let us look at particular features of the recent history of Mozambique and Angola in turn.

Mozambique

After the 1891 agreement the Portuguese, like other European countries, encouraged the development of their territories by Companies, which were given the right to administer their areas as well as to trade with them. The most important of these was the Mozambique Company whose rights included the territories of Manica and Sofala, which were only handed back to government control in 1942.

The economic development of Mozambique has been very closely connected with the British territories which surround it. The splendid capital city of Lourenço Marques has grown, chiefly because it is the main outlet for the products of Johannesburg and the whole

Transvaal, and the port of Beira to the north has developed chiefly because of the exports—especially of copper—from Rhodesia and the Congo. Another close connexion with the Union of South Africa is that much of the labour for the Johannesburg mines comes from Mozambique. Many young African men agree to work in the mines as wages there are much higher than in Mozambique. Usually they work for eighteen months at a time, and usually their purpose is to get enough money to get married and start a home.

As Mozambique was started as a colony for trade and not for settlement, there are only about 50,000 white people and 50,000 Asians and mulattos, compared with an African population which was reckoned in 1950 to be nearly six million. The vast majority of the African people are farmers. As well as subsistence crops, Africans have recently started to grow cotton on a large scale and this now provides the most valuable export of Mozambique. The profits which come from it may have some effect in reducing the number of Africans who seek employment in other colonies. Many Africans are also employed on the railways, and in banks, shops and schools. The education of the African people has been mainly the task of the Roman Catholic missions who have been given financial help by the Portuguese government, but there are also some state schools. Although primary schools are fairly numerous there are far fewer opportunities for higher education than in most of the other territories of Africa. Very few secondary schools exist and there is no University College.

Occasionally attempts have been made to increase the European population of Mozambique, but generally the Portuguese government has been very cautious about this, and only comparatively skilled and wealthy Europeans have been permitted to settle. There are no restrictions upon Indians entering Mozambique, and many of those who have entered are Goans who are often clerks, artisans, or domestic servants.

Angola

After the partition treaties defining Angola's boundaries, the

Portuguese slowly extended their authority inland over the African tribes. Sometimes the process was peaceful; sometimes—as with the Kunahamas in the south—it was not.

Unlike the Congo to the north, Angola has no long navigable rivers, and the need for railways was therefore particularly important. The map shows that there are several lines in Angola, but the main one is the Benguela Railway which connects with others to cross the African continent from the Atlantic to the Indian Ocean after twisting and turning through the Congo and Rhodesia to Mozambique. This line was suggested and financed by a British Company named 'The Tanganyika Concessions Ltd'. It began in 1903 and was completed in 1929 at a cost of £13 million. Its purpose was to provide an outlet for the copper of the Katanga region, and in this it has succeeded. As a result Benguela and the nearby port of Lobito provide the main gateway to Angola as well as to the Upper Congo. Another result of the railway was that the Portuguese in 1927 made Nova Lisboa, which was situated on the line in a central position, the new capital instead of Loanda. In fact, however, Loanda still remains the largest city, and one of the most pleasant on the west coast of Africa.

The main products which have been developed in Angola are coffee, maize and sugar. More recently diamonds have become an important export and there is hope that oil may be found near Loanda.

The total population of Angola in 1950 was about four million, which is very small in comparison with Angola's size. As a result of this small population labour is very carefully controlled; no one, for example, is allowed to go to the Johannesburg mines. Also European settlement has had more encouragement than in Mozambique, and numbers about 80,000.

Despite Portugal's efforts to shield Angola from 'the wind of change', nationalism, influenced by events in the Congo, led to serious rebellion in 1961.

CHAPTER 13

SOUTH AFRICA

POLITICAL DEVELOPMENT

When the South Africa Act had been passed, the Governor-General offered the vital position of Prime Minister to General Botha. The choice was good. In private life this fearless soldier was happily married and when away from home he always finished his day by talking to his wife on the telephone before he went to bed. In his political life he was tolerant, dignified and wise. Above all he was determined to break down the divisions between the Dutch and the English. Throughout his ministry, the man upon whom Botha chiefly relied for advice was his old friend General Smuts, who became a member of the Cabinet. Smuts, in many ways, was the opposite of Botha. He was brilliant, impatient and rather cold; he much preferred to deal with paper and schemes than with men and women; he was nicknamed 'Slim (crafty) Jannie'. Yet he and Botha stood together as a team until Botha's death, each supplying what the other lacked. Smuts supplied many bright ideas, but it was Botha's warm and simple greatness which held the Union together.

Botha led the South African Party, and at first his policy of conciliation worked well enough in Cape Colony, the Transvaal and in Natal. The main difficulty came from the Orange Free State where many of the Afrikaners, or Dutch, wished to keep themselves separate from the English. Among those who desired this permanent separation was Hertzog, who had accepted the post of Minister of Justice in Botha's government. But in 1912 he split away to form a party of his own—the National Party—which aimed at keeping Afrikaner and English development in South Africa separate. He was supported by the more extreme Afrikaners and especially by his own province, the Orange Free State.

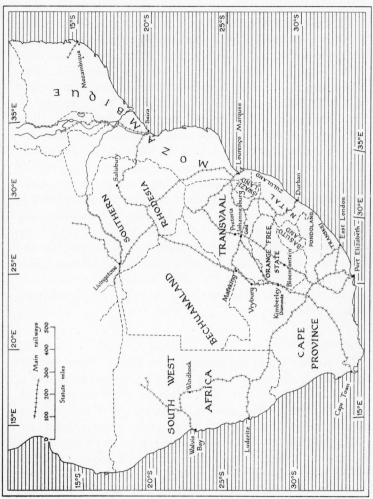

Map 14. South Africa today.

The Great War (1914–18)

The dislike which some Afrikaners had of being connected with the British showed itself in 1914 when Britain and Germany declared war on one another. Botha told Britain that South Africa could defend itself, and offered to conquer German South West Africa. Considering how recently the Boers and British had been at war with each other this was a remarkable offer. It was too remarkable for many Afrikaners in the Transvaal and Orange Free State. There, rebellion broke out and a brief—but fierce—civil war took place because so many Afrikaners disliked being involved in a British war. The rebels were defeated and treated generously. Then, early in 1915, the campaign against German South West Africa began. Botha himself took command, and in a few months the Germans, who were heavily outnumbered, were forced to accept unconditional surrender. South African troops then went to East Africa and Europe, and Botha and Smuts were both present at, and signed, the final peace treaty at Versailles between Britain and Germany. The importance of South Africa was further increased when the government of South West Africa was given to her under mandate from the League of Nations.

Post-war difficulties

In 1919 Botha died and Smuts took his place as Prime Minister and leader of the South African Party. He was not as popular as Botha had been, and soon new troubles came which made him more disliked. These troubles arose in the mining city of Johannesburg, which stood on the richest gold reef in the world and provided most of South Africa's wealth. Rich and poor, black and white, lived in the city and worked in the mines. On several previous occasions violent labour disputes had occurred, but in 1922 the greatest dispute of all began and the miners tried to take over the mines. Smuts himself took control of affairs in Johannesburg and started a full-scale war on the rebels. Battles raged through the city, whole streets were destroyed and 800 people were killed before the miners gave in and returned to work. But the price of victory had been high, and when Hertzog said that Smuts' footsteps 'dripped with blood' there were many people who were inclined to agree with him. As a result, in the 1924 elections, the South African Party was defeated and Smuts ceased to be Prime Minister.

Hertzog and the Nationalists

Hertzog, as leader of the Nationalist Party, took Smuts' place. His election was a sign, not only of Smuts' unpopularity, but also of the feelings of the Afrikaners. They were outnumbered by the English, and they saw the British Empire as a subtle organisation which might swallow them up. They were determined not to be swallowed. Therefore, they insisted on the use of the Afrikaans language and obtained its official recognition in 1925; they opposed the use of the Union Jack as their flag and nearly provoked a civil war, and they issued stamps which no longer showed the king's head. There was also a strong wish to break with Britain altogether and form a Republic. But at the Imperial Conference of 1926, attended by all the Prime Ministers of British Dominions, General Hertzog decided to remain within the Commonwealth and accepted the definition that Britain and her Dominions were 'autonomous (self-governing) communities within the British Empire, equal in status, in no way subordinate one to another ..., though united by a common allegiance to the Crown'. Hertzog told the people of South Africa that this meant complete independence, and he was right. Although the allegiance to the king remained, and although South Africans were still British subjects, they were independent in all other ways with no legal restrictions upon their ability to make laws or upon their dealings with other countries. The Governor-General became the representative of the king, while the High Commissioner became the representative of the British government.

The United Government of Hertzog and Smuts

In the early 1930's there was a slump all over the world; in other words, there was a shortage of money, a decrease in production and more unemployment. To help South Africa at this difficult time Smuts agreed to join with Hertzog as deputy Prime Minister in a United Government composed of the Nationalist and South African Parties. Although Hertzog and Smuts succeeded in getting on together, the more extreme members of both parties did not. So two new parties began. The extreme pro-British members broke away to form the Dominion Party, and the extreme pro-Afrikaner members, led by Dr Malan, broke away to form the Purified Nationalist Party. This was to become increasingly important.

Meanwhile the United government remained in power and prosperity began to return. Hertzog took the opportunity to push forward the policy of separating Europeans from Africans, and in 1936 the right to vote was taken from educated Africans in Cape Province and a system of indirect representation in the Union Parliament was substituted.

The Second World War (1939–45)

At the end of the 1930's the United government came to a dramatic end over the question of whether South Africa should enter the war against Germany. Smuts thought that it should. Hertzog thought that it should not. Many Afrikaners were sympathetic towards Germany so the debate was close, but by a small majority Smuts won. Hertzog promptly resigned and South Africa joined the war. Her strategic position, and the troops which were supplied for campaigns in Abyssinia and elsewhere, were of immense importance to Britain and her allies.

The triumph of Malan and the Nationalists

Meanwhile the opposition to Smuts grew. Hertzog died in 1943 and the Nationalist Party was then led by the more extreme Dr Malan. In 1948 he won the election. He won it because he was so typical of the Afrikaners whom he represented. Born in 1874 in Cape Province he became a Doctor of Divinity at Utrecht in the Netherlands and then returned to South Africa as a minister in the Dutch Reformed Church. Then, in 1915, he became editor of a nationalist newspaper and later entered politics. He was sincerely convinced of the rightness of his own aims and moved deliberately towards them with the full support of the Afrikaners. The main point of Malan's policy was to separate the African people from the white people of South Africa in as many ways as possible—the policy of 'apartheid'. Secondly, the Nationalist Party were determined to increase their majority by using every possibility the constitution offered to raise the proportion of Afrikaner votes. One result was the passing of the Constitution of the Senate Act (1955) which increased the membership of the Senate in such a way that the Nationalist Party would be certain of a majority there. Since then the Senate has recognised the right of the Union Parliament to place the Coloured people of Cape Province on a separate voting system.

Dr Malan was succeeded in 1954 by Mr Strijdom, who was succeeded in 1958 by Dr Verwoerd. Throughout this time the Nationalist Party has increased its power and appears to have become more extreme. Dr Verwoerd, who has been a professor of psychology, a Johannesburg newspaper editor, a Senator, and the Minister of Native Affairs, said shortly after becoming Prime Minister that he intended to continue the apartheid policy in order to ensure 'happiness, security, and stability for both Bantu and Whites'. Following a referendum in 1960 South Africa became a Republic, and in 1961 it withdrew from the Commonwealth as its policy of apartheid met with growing dislike.

ECONOMIC DEVELOPMENT

There have been three main stages in the economic development of South Africa—the agricultural stage, the mining stage, and the industrial stage.

Until the later part of the nineteenth century South Africa was an agricultural country, and its people—both African and European— were farmers. Most of the African farming was of a subsistence nature; the grower intended to eat the food he grew, not sell it. European farmers, on the other hand, grew export crops to sell.

149

But agriculture did not bring South Africa the wealth that it has today. This came as a result of mineral discoveries. No other country has been so fortunate as South Africa in this respect. Diamonds, gold and recently uranium have been discovered at convenient times and they have brought huge profits. Gold mining on the Witwatersrand has already brought South Africa three thousand million pounds and new mines in the Orange Free State are only just coming into production. Recently, uranium, which is important for atomic energy, has been developed as a by-product.

Today, the most valuable products of South Africa do not come from her mines but from her industries. These are varied. One of the largest industrial concerns is the Iron and Steel Corporation, started in 1927. Another important organisation is the Industrial Development Corporation, started in 1940. As a result of her rapid industrial growth there are now very few manufactured goods which South Africa does not produce.

The railways of South Africa have developed to connect the main mining and industrial centres with the ports. The roadways, the chief of which are tarmacadam double carriage-ways, are the best in Africa.

SOCIAL DEVELOPMENT

There are four main racial groups in South Africa: Africans, Europeans, Coloureds and Indians.

The Africans are easily the largest of these groups. They number about nine million and the great majority are Bantu. About 10 % of the land in the Union has been set aside for them, the chief reserves being those of Zululand, Pondoland, the Transkei and Vendaland. However, less than half the Bantu people actually live in these reserves. The majority work on European farms or in the cities, where African suburbs have developed such as Sophiatown on the outskirts of Johannesburg. Up to a point African education has been encouraged, and until 1954 it was managed by the Provinces. Then, the Bantu Education Act placed all Bantu education under the control of the Union government, which is planning to reorganise the Bantu educational system to give greater emphasis to practical subjects.

The general policy of the Nationalist government has been to keep the African people in a separate and subordinate social, economic, and constitutional position compared with the Europeans. This policy of separation, or 'apartheid', does not necessarily involve ill-treatment, but it has some very unpopular features from the African point of view. One of the most unpopular is the demand that all Africans shall carry a pass book, and in 1960 this led to a serious incident at Sharpeville, near Cape Town, when many Africans were shot by police who fired on a crowd. General disturbances amongst Africans throughout the Union followed, but these were vigorously suppressed by the government despite strong world-wide feeling in sympathy with the African people.

There are about three million Europeans in the Union. They control its affairs and hold 90 % of its land. The Afrikaners have become the greatest influence and are mainly responsible for the emphasis on 'apartheid' and demands for complete separation from Britain. The people of English origin are most numerous in Natal. Because there are two European groups, there are also two European languages—Afrikaans and English.

The Coloureds number over a million and live mainly in Cape Province. They have very little African blood because their ancestors rarely married with the Bantu. Until recently they were allowed a vote and were regarded in many ways as part of the European society. Mr Strijdom's government, however, took a stricter attitude and removed them from the European voting roll.

Most of the 400,000 Indians live in Natal, which they entered in the last part of the nineteenth century at the invitation of the English settlers who wanted their help with the sugar plantations. Since 1911 immigration has been forbidden, and attempts to restrict their trading have led to many complaints by the Indian government. In the early days the chief agitator on behalf of the Indians was Mahatma Gandhi, whose policy of civil disobedience (deliberately breaking laws without using violence) has been used many times since.

Beside and within the Union are Basutoland, Swaziland and Bechuanaland, which are known as the High Commission Territories.

When the South Africa Act was passed, both the British and South African governments expected that these areas would one day become part of the Union. The Union wanted this but the African people of the territories strongly opposed it. Since Hertzog's policy of segregation began, the British government has been reluctant to hand over the territories to the Union, although Nationalist governments have been very keen to control them.

Therefore these areas have continued to be administered by a High Commissioner. In each region there is a Resident Commissioner who uses a system of 'indirect' or 'parallel' rule through paramount chiefs and subchiefs. Since the 1930's political and social changes have been rapid.

Basutoland

This beautiful mountainous little country is populated by the Basuto people who were formed from clans scattered by the Zulu and Matabele raids. Britain took over its administration in 1884, but the Paramount Chief remained, and today the successors of the great King Moshesh still govern Basutoland. In 1960 Bereng Seeiso returned from Oxford University to be installed as ruler with the full approval of the Basuto National Council.

The Basutos are farmers, but it is necessary for most of the young men to go for a while to the Union mines to earn money.

Swaziland

The Africans of this tiny country seem to have broken away from the main body of the Bantu about 1750, and from that time were constantly at war with the Zulus. After the Boer War Swaziland came under British protection, and was included in the High Commission territories in 1907. The country is ruled by the king assisted by his traditional inner council (the Ligogo) and his larger council (the Libandhla).

Swaziland is richer than Basutoland and derives most of its wealth from asbestos mining.

Bechuanaland

This is a flat dry country where the main occupation is cattle rearing. Its great interest lies in its main tribe, the Bamangwato. Their reputation was made by Khama III who ruled from 1872 until 1923. As a youth he showed tremendous bravery—he once charged through the Matabele ranks alone—and as a chief he was remarkable for his unwavering support of the Christian faith. It was at his request that Bechuanaland became a British Protectorate in 1885. Unfortunately confusion arose over the succession when Seretse Khama aroused opposition in 1949 by marrying an English girl, but in 1961 he was permitted to return to political life.

SOUTH WEST AFRICA

As we have seen, the League of Nations gave the South African government the responsibility of administering South West Africa as a mandated territory in 1920. After the Second World War (1939–45) the League of Nations was replaced by the United Nations, and most of the mandated territories became trust territories under its supervision. However, the South African government demanded that the territory should become a province of the Union and refused to accept the United Nations' supervision. The United Nations, on the other hand, refused to accept South Africa's demands. The matter has not been settled, but in effect South West Africa is administered like one of the Provinces of the Union, and since 1949 it has sent elected members to the Union Parliament.

The chief export of South West Africa is minerals, especially diamonds, but most of the population are concerned with agriculture. The black pelt of the karakul sheep, introduced by the Germans in 1908, is particularly important.

Most of the African population live in the northern tribal territories where they are self-sufficient and carry on their traditional tribal government through chiefs. All the European population live in the south. The capital is Windhoek, which is joined to the ports of Walvis Bay and Luderitz by the railway.

CONCLUSION

This land of Africa was once called 'The Dark Continent'. If that was ever true it is true no more. From its palm-fringed coast on the Indian Ocean to the forests of the west, from the spacious grasslands of the veld to the desert in the north, Africa south of the Sahara is changing at a greater speed than perhaps any other country in history.

But Africa is big, too big to change completely in a generation, so some of its population have rushed far ahead of the rest. A young African may be a fully qualified doctor with a wife who can mix happily with anyone anywhere, while his brother may still be dressed in a blanket and live in a mud and wattle hut with numerous wives who carry bundles of sticks upon their backs. Yet once the change has started it will go on. For some it will be swift, for others slow, but Africa is on the move, and behind the movement are the resources of a great continent supported by capital and knowledge from Asia, Europe and the U.S.A. The future is bright with hope.

The future is also full of problems, for times of change are rarely peaceful times, and when a country changes as quickly as Africa the difficulties grow in proportion. Political independence has already come to many of its states, but the economic and social problems which are so real to every person on the continent remain. What is the best way to relieve the widespread poverty and ignorance? What is the best way for newly independent states to create confidence in their reliability and so attract the capital which is so vital for their development? What is the best way of settling relationships between races when they live side by side? These questions must be answered and no answer is likely to please everyone.

Africa has come a long way fast, and now its future lies balanced between possibilities and problems: both are as great as the continent itself.

INDEX

156

Natal, 72, 75, 144 f., 151
Negro, 7 f., 10, 14, 16, 26, 28, 36, 53
Niger, river, 7, 14, 17, 28, 50, 55, 57, 79 f., 102
Nigeria, 40, 53, 81 f., 86, 92 f., 101, 106 f., 120
Nile, 1, 6 f., 64, 86, 114
Nkrumah, Dr K., 99 f., 108
Nyangwe, 133
Nyasaland, 123 f.
Nyasa, Lake, 62, 63, 86 f.
Nyerere, J., 121

Ogowe, river, 103, 104
Oil Rivers, 39, 55, 57, 79
Oman, 45, 60 f.
Orange Free State, 72, 90 f., 144 f.
Orange River, 72, 88
Orange River Sovereignty, 72
Ordinance, 50th, 69, 70
Oubangi Chari, 104
Owen Falls, 114
Oyo, 39 f.

Park, Mungo, 55
Pemba, 30, 45, 121 f.
Persians, 18, 45
Peters, Carl, 84 f.
Philip, Dr J., 69
Phoenicians, 2, 6, 14, 21
Pinto, Serpa, 87
Portugal, General, 13, 21 f., 32 f., 42 f., 77, 89, 93 f., 139 f.
    Congo and Angola, 44, 139 f.
    East Africa, 12, 14, 19, 45 f., 60 f., 87, 139 f.
Prempeh, 79 f.
Prester John, 24
Pygmy, 10, 137

Queen Adelaide Province, 70

Rabai, 63
Rembann, Rev J., 63
Retief, Piet, 72

Rhodes, Cecil, 74 f., 88 f., 123 f.
Rhodesia, North, 74, 86 f., 89, 92, 115, 116, 123 f., 127, 139, 142
    South, 74, 86 f., 89, 115, 116, 123 f., 139, 142
Roberts, General, 90
Roberts, J. J., 53
Romans, 4 f.
Royal Geographical Society, 50, 64, 65
Ruanda, 13, 119 f., 138 f.
Rudolf, Lake, 8

Said, Seyyid, 60 f., 82
Salazar, Dr, 140
Salisbury, 88, 127
Samory, 79
Sao Thomé, 28, 124
Say, 79, 81
Schweitzer, Dr A., 104
Seif, Sultan bin, 45, 60
Seeiso, King, 152
Senegal River, 7, 14, 27, 38
    Country, 79, 102, 103, 106
Senegambia, 41
Shiré river, 65, 130
Sierra Leone, 26, 53 f., 58 f., 79, 99, 101, 106 f.
Smuts, General, 124, 144 f.
Sofala, 18, 27, 30, 31, 141
Sokoto, 17
Songhai, 16 f.
Sophiatown, 150
Sosso, 15,
Spain, 5, 15, 32 f., 36
Speke, Capt. J. H., 64, 65
Stanley, Sir H. M., 66, 67
Stellaland, 88
Strijdom, 149, 151
Sudan, 6 f., 14 f., 41, 50, 55, 58 f., 66, 79 f., 84, 102 f.
Suez, 10, 42, 51, 82
Swahili, people and language, 19, 119
Swaziland, 152 f.
Syria, 4 f.